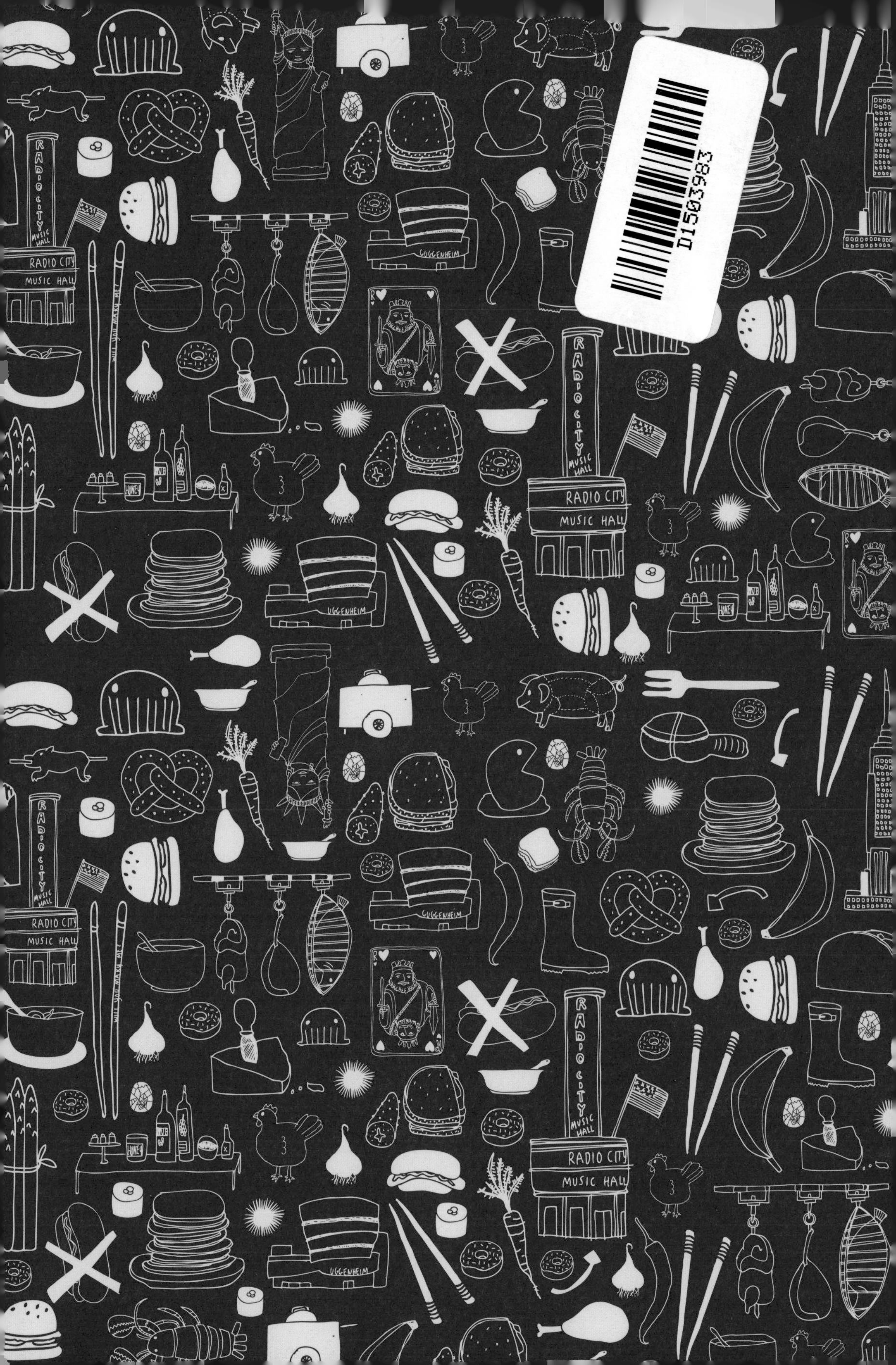
RADIO CITY MUSIC HALL
GUGGENHEIM
HONEY

RADIO CITY
MUSIC HALL
GUGGENHEIM
HONEY

# MUST EAT NYC

BUSINESS HOURS:
Mon. 11:00 am to 11:00 pm
Tues. 11:00 am to 11:00 pm
Wed. 11:00 am to 11:00 pm
Thur. 11:00 am to 11:00 pm
Fri. 11:00 am to 11:00 pm
Sat. 11:00 am to 11:00 pm
Sun. 11:00 am to 11:00 pm
Rem:
MUST EAT NYC
LANNOO
www.musteatnyc.com
FOR
ONLY
WE SUPPORT THE
9/11
MEMORIAL
Forever Changed. Forever Connected.
ZAGAT
2015
Rated on zagat.com
拉
PULL
UnionPay
银联
VISA
MasterCard
DISCOVER
JCB
RUNIN Out
Food-Fun-Fashion
Reviewed on tripadvisor.com
tripadvisor

# MUST EAT

## AN ECLECTIC SELECTION OF CULINARY LOCATIONS

LUC HOORNAERT
PHOTOGRAPHY: KRIS VLEGELS

LANNOO

DUN
Love
At
First
Bite
Love
At
First
Bite

## Scenes from the Battleship Gastronomica in NYC

"What's the purpose of your visit to NYC, sir?" asked the customs officer, minutes after I disembarked at JFK. "Um, well, lunch and dinner," I replied hesitantly. Three minutes later two custom officers were unpacking my luggage with the most sincere interest. I just barely avoided a full body cavity search. But I was telling the truth. I hadn't come to NYC to see the numerous mind-blowing landmarks, the fabulous museums or Broadway shows. I came here to eat, full stop, to give myself over to absolute gastronomical pleasure in all its forms.

As a child of the Old World, it seemed (for a long time) as if I were strapped to some sort of gastronomical chastity belt. Somehow it felt like my taste buds were not allowed to go all the way. My first eating experiences in NYC, however, completely liberated me from the burden of gastronomical history and even "proper gastronomy" which always seemed to peep over my shoulder like a black raven. Entertainment seems to be the hardest word to stomach in the Old World. Here I really found the best of both worlds. Old World focus, depth, and precision, coupled with a New World perspective, playfulness and vision. All of this was 30-odd years ago.

Being a full time importer of wine and high-end Japanese ingredients (in Belgium) gets me around the globe. Wherever I am I always try to scratch the surface to connect with the soul of local gastronomy and eating establishments. Nowhere else have I found more culinary bliss than in NYC.

*Must Eat NYC* is absolutely not a complete guide; the mere idea that a guide to NYC restaurants could ever be "complete" is utterly preposterous. The NYC food scene is a bit like a Borgesian encyclopedia; unimaginably endless and profoundly strange. *Must Eat NYC* highlights my personal favorites and features those dishes that touch me, embrace me, and make me feel like coming home.

I hope you enjoy and savor this guide as much as I did in its creation.

**Luc Hoornaert and Kris Vlegels**



*Thanks, dear Qurratul-ain, for your patience and strength.*
*You are the wind beneath my wings.*

*NYC in the rain, when?*

# CONTENT

UPTOWN WEST
Bronx
Manhattan
UPTOWN EAST
MIDTOWN WEST
MIDTOWN EAST
Queens
DOWNTOWN WEST
DOWNTOWN EAST
Brooklyn
Staten Island

## MIDTOWN EAST - 144



## DOWNTOWN WEST - 166



## DOWNTOWN EAST - 206

AVIS
TRUCK

GET HAPPY
HAVE A MARGARITA
I'M GONNA MAKE YOU A PIZZA YOU CAN'T REFUSE
42799
No Smoking
NO SLICES CASH ONLY
RESTROOM
Grimaldi's
Coal brick oven Pizzeria

1

# GRIMALDI'S

1 Front St., Brooklyn - NY 11201
T (718) 858-4300 - www.grimaldis-pizza.com
Open Mon-Thu: 11:30 a.m.-10:45 p.m., Fri: 11:30 a.m.-11:45 p.m., Sat: noon-11:45 p.m., Sun: noon-10:45 p.m.

Under the Brooklyn Bridge, of course on the Brooklyn side, you will always see a long line of people waiting in front of a very handsome building. These are the pizza enthusiasts waiting for a table at Grimaldi's, one of NY's best-loved pizzerias.

MIGUEL SANTOS
ATTORNEY

# Pizza Margherita

You can't reserve a table here and nope, they don't accept credit cards either.

One of the darkest days in Italian culinary history must have been when someone placed pineapple (from a can) for the first time on a pizza base and stuck it in the oven. Yet pizza Hawaii is the most popular pizza in Italy, thanks of course to the tourists. Pizza originated in the Mediterranean Sea area and people surmise that it began as a plate! In other words, people baked flat bread that was used as a tray. Everything that people wanted to eat was laid on it and only if one had an extremely big appetite, the 'plate' was also devoured. According to tradition, the Trojan hero Aeneas established the city of Lavinium on the spot where he devoured the empty plates (bread plates) himself out of hunger.

The Vikings also ate a type of pizza, namely a round-shaped bread with all sorts of ingredients on it which was baked in a type of pizza oven. It was only in the 17th century that pizza made its appearance in Naples, without the tomato sauce of course because at that time tomatoes were (erroneously) considered toxic. Tomatoes from South America were introduced in Europe around 1500 and were mostly a yellow variety. That is why the Italian name for tomato is pomo d'oro, which means "golden apple". The tomatoes that we see today were developed by means of cross-fertilization in the 18th century. The best-known pizza in those days was the Mastunicola, a pizza base decked with lard, pecorino, black pepper and basil.

Most people still consider pizza Margherita *the* most authentic pizza. It was created by Raffaele Esposito, one of the best-known pizza makers in Naples. He had the honor of making a pizza for King Umberto I and his wife Margherita. His chauvinism inspired him to create a pizza with the colors of the Italian flag (tomato sauce, buffalo mozzarella and basil) and that's how pizza Margherita was born.

In 1941, when Patsy Grimaldi was just ten years old, he lived in the Italian part of Harlem where he learned the skills of pizza making. Patsy dreamed of having his own pizza restaurant in Manhattan, but there was one problem: You can only achieve the wonderful thin and crispy bottom and crust in an oven that ideally reaches a temperature of approximately 932° F. That is only possible in an oven fueled by charcoal or coal. His dream was shattered because Manhattan didn't permit new construction of such ovens. But in Brooklyn that was still possible, and so the location was moved to the current address! The oven weighs 25 tons and runs at a toasty but comfortable temperature of approximately 1202° F. (still pretty damn hot). Fresh dough, a daily delivery of super-fresh mozzarella and fresh San Marzano tomatoes do the rest.

MERICAN
EAGLE.

2

# HIBINO

333 Henry St. (Atlantic & Pacific), Cobble Hill, Brooklyn - NY 11201
T (718) 260-8052 - www.hibino-brooklyn.com

Open Mon-Thu: noon-2:30 p.m. and 5:30 p.m.-10:00 p.m., Fri: noon-2:30 p.m. and 5:30 p.m.-10:30 p.m.
Sat: 5:30 p.m.-10:30 p.m., Sun: 5:30 p.m.-10:00 p.m.

This walk-in restaurant specializes in traditional and contemporary sushi, Kyoto style tapas known as *obanzai*, and homemade tofu. The latter is an enormous task, because tofu is not the simplest dish to make, nor is it the most popular.

HIBINO

# Freshly Made Tofu, with grated ginger and scallions, soy-dashi sauce

The first piece of evidence of the existence of tofu was a stone tablet in the grave of Han, illustrating how to make tofu. It was a poem, a tribute to tofu, written by Su Ping in 1500 BC. Obviously, we can never be sure whether this was genuine, but the fact is that tofu reached Japan via China. Kento priests, who during the Nara period (710-794 AD) traveled to China to study Buddhism, brought back the tofu-making technique to the land of the rising sun. Tofu is a source of protein and the word tofu was used for the first time in Japan in the diary of Shinto priest Nakaomi, who used tofu as an offering on the altar.

It was not until 1489 that the word tofu actually spread throughout Japan by means of Kanji (Chinese letters) and became popular among the Samurai and the noble class. During the Edo period (1603-1867), tofu also became popular among common people. There was even a cookbook printed in 1782, *Tofu Hyakuchin,* that became a bestseller.

In the USA, the first tofu business was established in 1895 in San Francisco by Hirata & Co. Tofu is very healthy and when it is prepared with top ingredients, it is delicious. They certainly demonstrate this at Hibino where they serve tofu very honorably and with a quality level that I've rarely tasted outside of Japan. Go and discover this hidden gem on Cobble Hill.

COOK

3

# VINEGAR HILL HOUSE

72 Hudson Ave. (Water&Front), Brooklyn - NY 11201
T (718) 522-1018 – www.vinegarhillhouse.com

Open Mon-Thu: 6:00 p.m.-11:00 p.m., Fri: 6:00 p.m.-11:30 p.m.,
Open Sat: 10:30 a.m.-3:30 p.m. and 6:00 p.m.-11:30 p.m., Sun: 10:30 a.m.-3:30 p.m. and 5:30 p.m.-11:00 p.m.

You will find Vinegar Hill slightly north of Dumbo. In this part of Brooklyn, the waterfront still has a strong industrial tone and walking from the nearest subway station you are confronted with urban raw. In contrast, Vinegar Hill House provides a very warm and cozy atmosphere.

## Octopus, wild leek, tahini, celery, golden raisin

It is a cross between Nellie's restaurant in Little House on the Prairie and Freemans, a hip restaurant in the Lower East Side.

There is a very pleasant atmosphere here, reminiscent of Nellie's, but the food is without a doubt much better. Rough wooden furniture, interior illumination and the occasional melted candle wax give the place a *back-in-time look,* reminiscent of a sailors dive in a great Jacques Brel song.

The showpiece is an oven fired only by wood. Such an appliance provides depth and flavor to some very simply looking dishes and, moreover, looks like an altar. Many dishes are prepared in this oven and it makes them ever tastier, similar to the taste achieved by using a Japanese robatayaki. Here, the kitchen team has given the level of expression a boost, more so than it did at Freemans. There the food was more stylized; here it's more about taste and culinary expression and some dishes have become local legends, like the pork chop.

The dishes are created intuitively and that is what you'll notice when you look at the menu. At first glance, the pairings are not self-evident, but when you taste them, they work wonderfully. Vinegar Hill House is a restaurant with a high feel-good factor and an exceptional vibe, which carries over into the garden. Finish your perfect day (after a pleasant walk from Manhattan, for example) by showing up at this place around opening time. From that moment, let the evening slowly go by. You'll have no regrets.

French Louie
Our garden is OPEN
AMIGOS

4

# FRENCH LOUIE

320 Atlantic Ave. (between Smith and Hoyt St.), Boerum Hill, Brooklyn - NY 11201
T (718) 935-1200 – www.frenchlouienyc.com
Open Mon-Thu: 11:30 a.m.-10:30 p.m., Fri: 11:30 a.m.-11:30 p.m., Sat: 10:00 a.m.-11:30 p.m., Sun: 10:00 a.m.-10:00 p.m.

In the small neighborhood of Boerum Hill, the story of Louis Seymour is still alive. Louis rode his donkey through the Adirondack Mountains and knew this area like the back of his hand. Moreover, he was a lumberjack, fisherman and hunter who preferred to live alone as a hermit in this incredibly beautiful region around Lake Placid.

# Snails 'Marchand de Vin'

Louis was born in 1832 in Ottawa, the French-speaking area of Canada. At a young age he ran away to the United States where he joined a circus. He lived off the abundance of natural resources in the expansive woods in the Adirondack Mountains. He was well-known in the area, mainly because twice a year he would come out of the woods to organize a hearty feast which he paid for with wild trout and beaver skins.

Louis, who was known as French Louie, was loved by everyone for his free spirit and positive attitude. Long after his death in 1915, he remains a source of inspiration for this beautiful 50-seat restaurant.

Doug Crowell and Ryan Angulo, the team behind the Buttermilk Channel Bistro in Carroll Gardens, opened this tribute to French Louie. This American bistro has built itself a solid reputation, promoting a kitchen that has deep roots in the local and regional cuisines and ingredients. Doug has literally manned every conceivable job in the restaurant and together with Ryan – after their Buttermilk Channel – they have positioned a high-flying restaurant on the map.

Buttermilk Channel, by the way, is the name of the small tidal strait between Brooklyn and Governors Island. Dairy farmers used to row their milk from Brooklyn to the markets in Manhattan along its course, and legend has it that when the channel crossing was very rough, their milk had churned to buttermilk by the time they reached Manhattan.

The resident chef, Justin Fulton, grew up in the Rocky Mountains of Colorado. He created a very attractive menu, making it hard to choose a dish. Contemporary, American cuisine with a touch of the exotic from the French areas and enclaves, such as New Orleans and Montreal. You can't get more French than escargots. Here they even make their own version called 'Escargots Marchand de Vin' and the name says it all. Beautiful, large snails in a rich and full Bordelaise sauce with oysters, home-pickled bacon and of course mushrooms. An immense dish.

The cozy garden is a fantastic place to sit, but doesn't quite succeed in allowing you to forget that you are still in Brooklyn and not close to French Louie.

ODETTA
Roberta's

5

# ROBERTA'S

261 Moore St. (between Bogart and White St.) - NY 11206
T (718) 417-1118 - www.robertaspizza.com
Open Mon-Fri: 11:00 a.m.-midnight, Sat-Sun: 10:00 a.m.-midnight

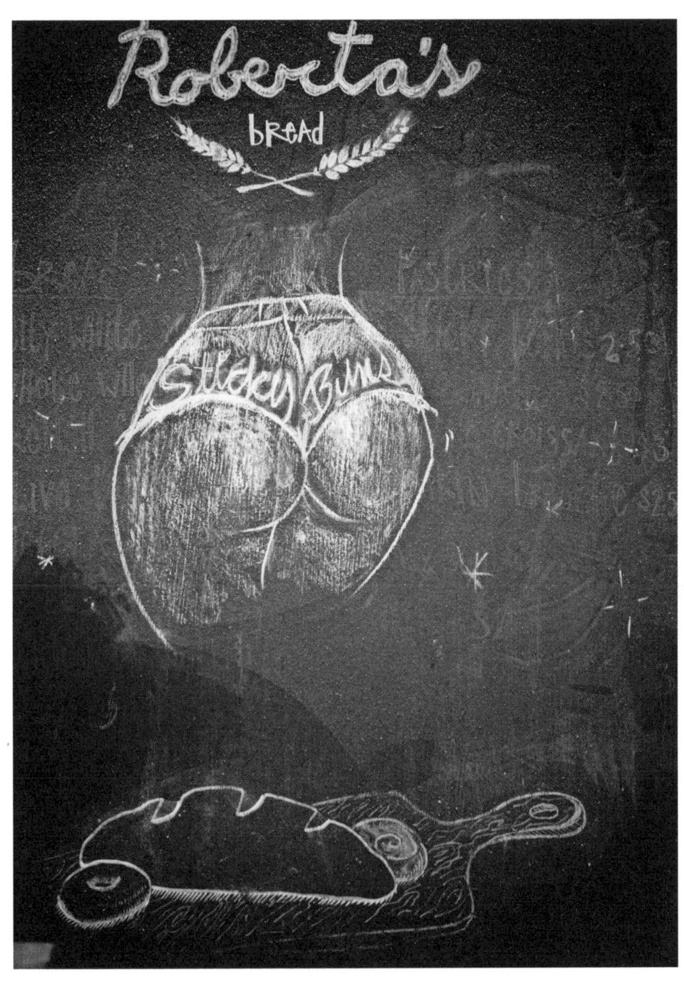


If you walk into a restaurant and see containers with Evergreen printed on them, a radio studio 'on the air' next to someone who is sitting to eat, a drawing of a scantily covered woman's buttocks that says *Nice Buns*, Mexican Christmas lights, a fire-spitting pizza oven, an ode to cowboys in love from *Brokeback Mountain* (drawn as a pizza face), and you hear *Master of Puppets* banging from the loud speakers, then you are probably sitting at Roberta's.

# The Cowabunga Dude pizza

the Mad MAx version of the traditional American diner

On a desolate street in Bushwick, you will find this Mad Max version of a classical American diner. It is a bit of a hipster utopia, but Roberta's means mainly fun, entertainment and damn good food. I absolutely do not want to reduce this restaurant to a pizzeria, but half the guests here eat pizza because it is really awesome. Perfect control of the dough mixture, dripping with mozzarella, does the trick according to Lauren Calhoun, the "pizza boss". The pizza toppings change constantly. I was a fan of their breakfast burrito pizza and of the Cheezus Christ, but right now, I am in my Cowabunga Dude pizza period: tomato, caciocavallo, pepperoni, mushrooms, onions, green peppers and olives. A real stunner.

I love coming to this place; there is always something to experience, and I repeat – the food is fantastically delicious. To their credit is the homemade duck ham and pastrami sandwich, and if tartare is suggested, nothing can hold me back. All the artisanship and skill come from chef Carlo Mirarchi, a thoroughbred chef who also runs Blanca, the star joint next door. Roberta's is top by all standards.

MIGHTY QUINN'S
PIZZA MOTO
PIZZA MOTO
FORT GREENE FLEA
SMORGASBURG
WILLIAMSBURG
BROOKLYN FLEA
TOTE BAGS $10
MUGS $5
SMORGASBURG
SMORGASBURG
ETHIOPIAN
CONSUMER.

6

# SMORGASBURG

Smorgasburg Williamsburg, East River State Park, 90 Kent Ave (at N. 7th St.)., Brooklyn – NY 11211

Open Sat: 11:00 a.m.-6:00 p.m.

Smorgasburg Prospect Park, Prospect Park, Well House Dr., Brooklyn – NY 11225

Open Sun: 11:00 a.m.-6:00 p.m.

www.smorgasburg.com.

Every time I walk the streets of NYC after a harsh winter and here and there espy Japanese cherry blossoms announcing the tide of spring, I cry with joy. It is Smorgasburg time again!

BonXChouie
Fried Anchovies
Fresh Sandwiches
$10 Grilled Salmon
Cornmeal-Crusted Cod
Sambora $4
people's pops
ICE POPS
$3.50
Apple Rosewater
APRICOT RASPBERRY
Strawberry Lemongrass
SHAVE ICE
LEMON BASIL
$2.50
PLUM ORANGE BLOSSOM
Made with REAL, LOCAL FRUIT
VERMONT MAPLE LEMONADE
Organic Vegetable
QUEEN COBRA THAI
ICE CREAM SANDWICHES
menu
tips for the girls
CHAMOYADA
(chah-moh-yada)
Tamarind candy
COLD WATER! $1
BIG BEAR HUGS
COCONUT

# Local vendors

Smorgasburg is an initiative of Brooklyn Flea, a company that specializes in organizing large flea markets throughout the entire east coast of the US. Because more and more food stands joined and offered their services, they decided that it was time for a new initiative. Smorgasburg (a combination of Smorgasbord and Williamsburg) is one of the biggest weekly food events in the US.

More than one hundred food stands offer their specialties at this Woodstock for food lovers. Some stands are very modest, while others come out ablaze in visual spectacle. Just as NYC is a cultural melting pot, so is this NYC version of the famous Jamaa-el-Fnaa in Marrakesh – a real gastronomical melting pot.

At times only the breathtaking view of the Manhattan skyline and the Brooklyn Bridge betray the fact that you are not in some exotic *souk*, but in Brooklyn. Every time I am set loose here, I reach my limit... and want more! And that is perfectly permissible, because anyone who can resist is not a real foodie.

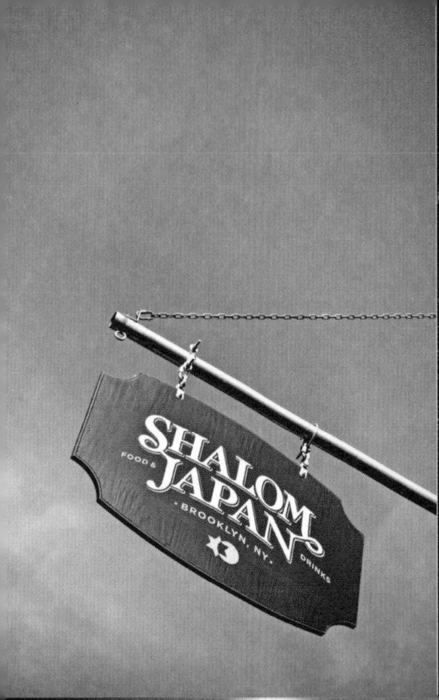

SHALOM JAPAN
FOOD & DRINKS
BROOKLYN, NY.

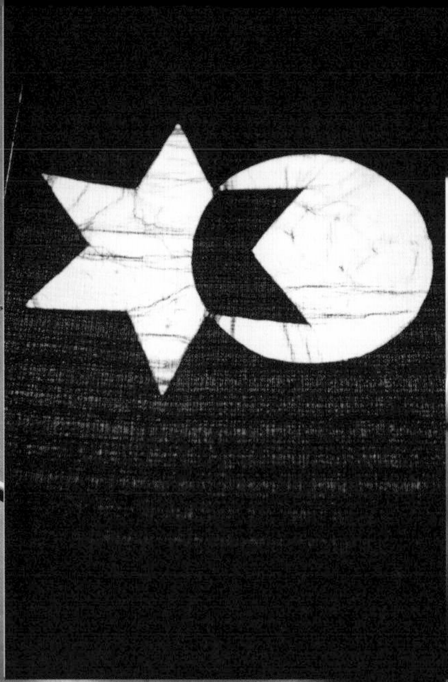

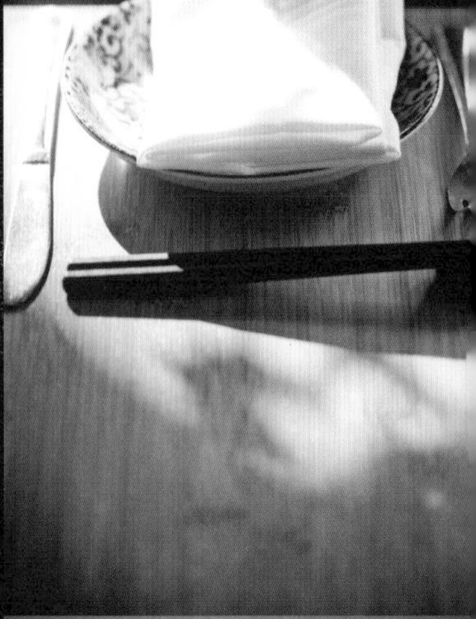

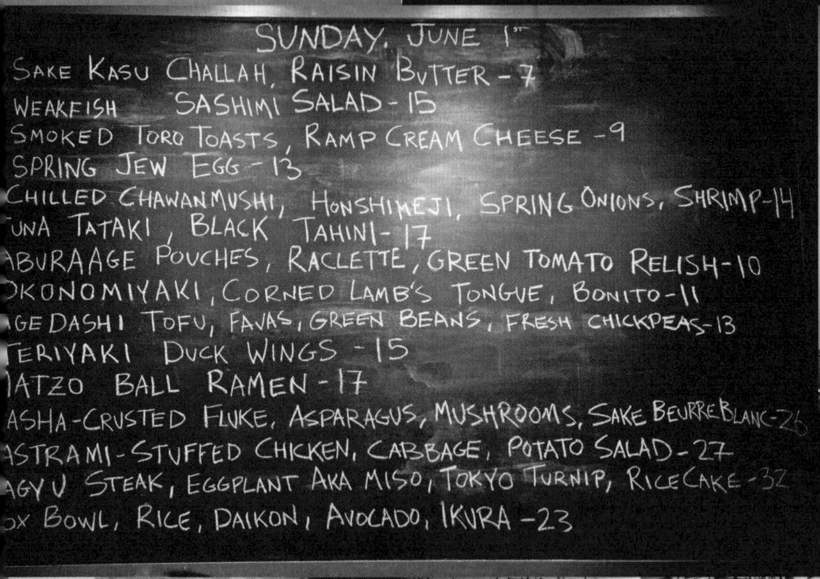

SUNDAY, JUNE 1ST
SAKE KASU CHALLAH, RAISIN BUTTER - 7
WEAKFISH SASHIMI SALAD - 15
SMOKED TORO TOASTS, RAMP CREAM CHEESE - 9
SPRING JEW EGG - 13
CHILLED CHAWANMUSHI, HONSHIMEJI, SPRING ONIONS, SHRIMP - 14
UNA TATAKI, BLACK TAHINI - 17
ABURAAGE POUCHES, RACLETTE, GREEN TOMATO RELISH - 10
OKONOMIYAKI, CORNED LAMB'S TONGUE, BONITO - 11
GEDASHI TOFU, FAVAS, GREEN BEANS, FRESH CHICKPEAS - 13
TERIYAKI DUCK WINGS - 15
ATZO BALL RAMEN - 17
ASHA-CRUSTED FLUKE, ASPARAGUS, MUSHROOMS, SAKE BEURRE BLANC - 26
ASTRAMI-STUFFED CHICKEN, CABBAGE, POTATO SALAD - 27
AGYU STEAK, EGGPLANT AKA MISO, TOKYO TURNIP, RICE CAKE - 32
OX BOWL, RICE, DAIKON, AVOCADO, IKURA - 23

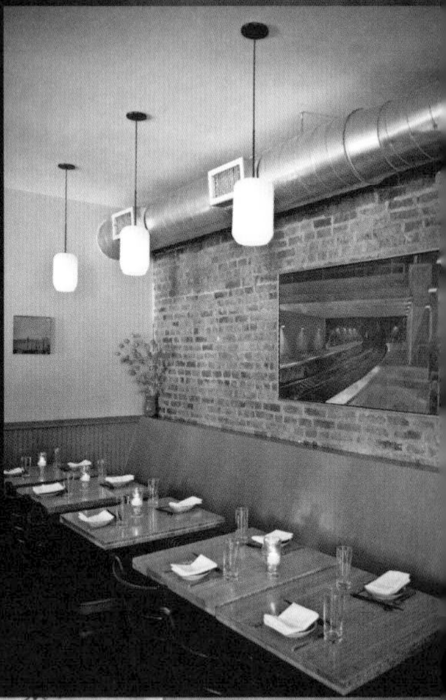

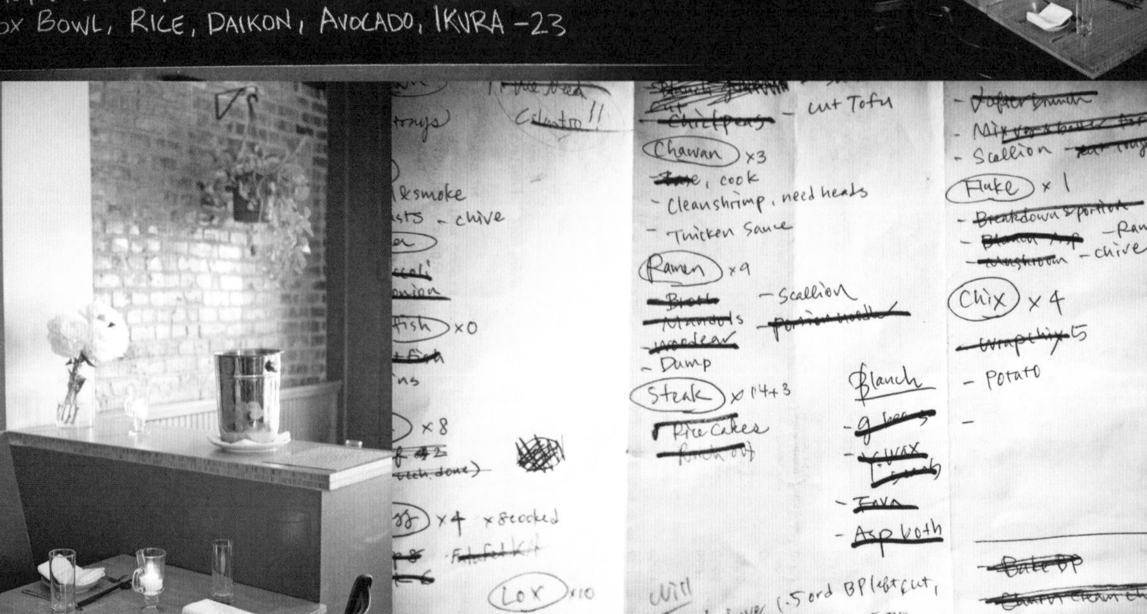

7

# SHALOM JAPAN

310 S 4th St. (@Rodney Street) - NY 11211
T (718) 388-4012 - www.shalomjapannyc.com

Open Tue-Wed: 5:30 p.m.-10:00 p.m., Thu-Fri: 5:30 p.m.-11:00 p.m., Sat-Sun: brunch 11:00 a.m.-3:00 p.m., Sat: dinner 5:30 p.m.-11:00 p.m., Sun: dinner 5:30 p.m.-10:00 p.m.

Sawako Okochi and Aaron Israel, both chefs at Shalom Japan, are gastronomical jacks-of-all-trades and that has a lot to do with their cultural origins. Sawako, born in Hiroshima, came to NYC in 2000 via Texas. Aaron, who grew up in Great Neck, has worked in some of the most acclaimed culinary establishments.

# Okonomiyaki, salt-cured lamb's tongue, bonito flakes

Together, they are not only a couple, but also Shalom Japan, a most unusual name for a restaurant. The name, by the way, came from a kosher restaurant on 22 Wooster Street in Soho, where Miriam Mizakura, a Japanese Jewess sang, danced and cracked Jewish jokes. She served gefilte sashimi and challah singing *Hava Nagila*. Unfortunately this restaurant stopped existing some 10 odd years ago.

It is easy to find. A few blocks from the Williamsburg Bridge, you follow the sounds of hip-hop music typically coming from the youngsters playing basketball on the court in the Rodney Park Playground and it is directly on the other side.

This restaurant is more than a unique collaboration; it is actually the melting together of two separate cultures, cooking experiences and a passion for fine food. This has resulted in mature, but playful dishes that show great respect for both cultures. At first glance, the Jewish gastronomic culture does not seem to share the same level of refinement as the supremely refined Japanese food culture, but somehow the collaboration works brilliantly. A major advantage in making this work is the immense selection of fresh and dry products available in this city.

Making a food choice is my most difficult task in this restaurant, because as a Japanese food freak, I am naturally very curious about what I get in a fusion with the Jewish kitchen. Their version of one of my favorite lunch dishes in Japan, okonomiyaki, is indeed very successful and perhaps an improvement of the original. With the addition of a nearly candied lamb's tongue, I enjoyed the essential, full texture that you get in okonomiyaki.

Okonomiyaki is a popular lunch dish in the Land of the Rising Sun. It might be described as somewhere between a pancake and a hearty omelet filled with leek, Chinese cabbage and delicious nagaimo (yams); it is all topped with Japanese mayonnaise and otafuku sauce (a sort of sweet Japanse Worcestershire), and on top of that, you'll find a bit of grated hana katsuo and ginger. This fast, delicious and sexy lunch is glorious and shows a lesser known aspect of the very diverse Japanese kitchen.

As a huge fan of black sesame and tuna, I was very impressed by the tuna tataki with black tahini. Lovely, barely cooked tuna in a circle of black tahini is once again a very smart fusion. Black sesame is actually used a lot in Japanese desserts and this dish is an upscale version of the nearly classical black sesame-crusted tuna.

When you go out, take a good look at the Star of David and the Rising Sun that flow into each other. For me, this is one of the few establishments that actually understands the meaning of fusion cooking.

## 8

# TRAIF

229 S 4th St. (between Havemeyer and Roebling St.) - NY 11211
T (347) 844-9578 - www.traifny.com
Open Tue-Thu: 6:00 p.m.-midnight, Fri-Sat: 6:00 p.m.-1:00 a.m., Sun: 6:00 p.m.-midnight

On the way to Traif I asked directions from one of the many Chassidic Jews walking on Havemeyer. My best Yiddish (which sounds not utterly dissimilar from Flemish) was almost adequate, but then I realized that traif is the Yiddish word for non-kosher food, which is forbidden according to strict Jewish dietary laws.

# A celebration of pork

When I arrived, I noticed that the small, delicate logo on the door pictured a cute little piglet with a very small heart. I find this to be very subtle humor for this neighborhood and even more so because one of the couple/owners, Jason Marcus and Heather Heuser... is Jewish. (This is, in fact, the only way they can pull off this caper.)

Jason is not just any cook; Le Bernardin and Eleven Madison Park stand out on his CV. This philosopher, by the way, stands alongside his cooks, working in the tiny kitchen. The menu is very much tied to the season and therefore it constantly changes. The concept here is to order small and big dishes that you can share with other people at your table.

I think that Jason has been rather underrated as a chef (maybe it's the cuteness of the concept), and consequently, Traif is a rather underrated restaurant. Every meal I have enjoyed in Traif was a direct hit! His ability to combine flavors is a refined development. If I see how busy the place is, then I know that by now a lot people have discovered Jason's fantastic dishes.

Jason and Heather met while working together in a restaurant in San Diego. When they fell in love, they set out on a clear course: travel through Europe, go live in NY and then open a restaurant called Traif. In Barcelona they had sat at a bar called Xix (pronounced "chicks" in Catalan). Sometime later, when they had already established Traif, premises down the street (at 241 4th St.) became available. They thought back to their experience at Xix, and voilà, Xixa was conceived. Their new establishment was designed in a cool and esthetic manner and Xixa (pronounced "shiksa" in Spanish) is a playful reference to the cozy bar in Barcelona and to the fact that Heather is Jason's "shiksa", which in Yiddish means a non-Jewish woman (typically a girlfriend). Xixa, nominally a "Mexican" restaurant, can be thought of as a bit like a transposition of Traif to Mexico City. Xixa has an unbelievably good vibe and atmosphere plus the extra touch of cocktails and an impressive wine list. I am an absolute fan of Jason's kitchen and of Heather's sense for detail and service. (And their wicked sense of humor.) A top combination.

OUR OWN
Peter Luger
STEAK HOUSE
SAUCE
HO
255 NORTH
GREAT N
516 487
luger.c
NO SMOKING

9

# PETER LUGER

178 Broadway (@Driggs) - NY 11211
T (718) 387-7400 - www.peterluger.com
Open Mon-Thu: 11:45 a.m.-9:45 p.m., Fri-Sat: 11:45 a.m.-10:45 p.m., Sun: 12:45 p.m.-9:45 p.m.

Some restaurants – fortunately, for the most part – have a Zagat Award hanging high in a place of honor. When you open the door to this establishment, you see thirty Zagat Awards lined up in three rows of ten.

# Steak for two, creamed spinach, German baked potatoes, steaksauce

Yessiree, for thirty consecutive years, Peter Luger has been chosen as the best steakhouse in NYC by the most influential culinary guides in the US. And if you take a moment to look around the place and see the long wooden bar, the candlesticks and the simple tables, you can be sure of one thing: the awards are not for the decor!

Stepping in is also going back a bit in history. In 1887, Carl Luger opened here his Café Billiards & Bowling Alley. A few years later, in December 1903, the neighborhood fell under the shadow of the new Williamsburg Bridge and the local population was predominately German. Williamsburg was also suddenly more accessible and business got a boost. Peter Luger (1866-1941) was the owner and his nephew Carl was the chef. Already then, they made a name for themselves with the quality of their beef. In 1950, Peter's son decided to sell the restaurant in a public auction. Bad idea, because by then the neighborhood was populated by Chassidic Jews who had absolutely no interest in their rare beef and especially not in their German background. One of their best customers, Sol Forman, bought the building and business for $35,000. Forman had been taking his customers to eat at Peter Luger for 25 years and he was not about to change this cherished habit. So he simply bought the place and restored it to its glory. For sixty years of his life, Sol had been eating steak at Peter Luger five times per week and died at the age of 98 a happy man.

I cannot and will not reveal the secret of the quality of this place. It begins with the meat that has always been selected according to texture and taste, and is always USDA prime. Moreover, they have become masters in the skill of letting the meat ripen slowly by a dry-ageing method. Thirty years ago I ate here for the first time and already my then inexperienced taste buds told me that this is the place to experience something exceptionally delicious. A meal in this restaurant remains one the things I most look forward to whenever I am back in NYC. The perfect cooked steak, soft as butter yet tasteful, the unbelievably creamy and delicious spinach and the perfect baked potatoes, just like my grandmother used to make. Add a few generous spoonfuls of the unrivaled Peter Luger steak sauce, of which I always buy a few bottles to take home.

In Europe I find that La Table du Boucher in Mons is by far the best steakhouse on our continent. Luc Broutard, whom I call the cow whisperer, is the man who has awakened the entire European continent to beef cattle breeds, ageing and cooking techniques. My G-rated wet dream is to one day eat a Peter Luger USDA prime beef and a Holstein from Luc in the same meal. That for me would be heaven on earth...

FOOD LINE
BARRIER
Ball
WIDE MOUTH
Brooklyn
Brown Ale
Bronx

10

# FETTE SAU

354 Metropolitan Ave. (between N 4th and Roebling St.) - NY 11211
T (718) 963-3404 - www.fettesaubbq.com

Open Mon: 5:00 p.m.-11:00 p.m., Tue-Thu: noon-11:00 p.m., Fri-Sat: noon-midnight, Sun: noon-11:00 p.m.

Williamsburg is a trendy neighborhood where hobos and graffiti have to compete with gourmet cheese stores, extravagant music happenings, topnotch trendy retail stores and superior restaurants. Some parts of this area actually remind me a bit of Berlin.

SHORT PLATE
RIB
BRISKET
SQUARE-CUT CHUCK
SHANK

# Smoked beef brisket, hand-pulled Berkshire pork, housemade Berkshire sausage

From the sidewalk, it is not so easy to spot Fette Sau, but fortunately there is one way of recognizing it, which you cannot miss – the oh-so-wonderful smoky smell of barbecue that seems to linger outside its gate, which sports a tiny, discreet signboard, and entices you inside. You would never suspect that one of NYC's finest barbecue restaurants is located here.

The building that accommodates Fette Sau was previously a garage and in terms of the infrastructure, it still looks like one. A long driveway where simple picnic tables stand leads to the restaurant. The restaurant is a real feast, even before you have had your first bite. The delicious smell that hangs in the air whets your appetite. They use red and white oak, apple, cherry, peach and maple wood to achieve the complex aromas that penetrate the meat. All the wood, by the way, comes from upstate New York. Although Fette Brau – a beer brewed in the Pilsner style especially for them – flows abundantly from the taps, the handgrips of which are old butcher knives, and there is no need for an apéritif due to these delicious aromas. My mouth is watering already.

Beer, by the way, is the strong point of Fette Sau, but that will surprise no one because the owners, Joe Carroll and Kim Barbour, have one of the best beer bars in NYC just on the other side of the street - the Spuyten Duyvil. Belgian beers and obscure mini-breweries are the specialty here. Spuyten Duyvil is a neighborhood in the Bronx, close to Spuyten Duyvil Creek, where the Hudson runs as wild as a spewing devil. History even tells us of a certain Anthony van Corlaer who in 1642 wanted to swim across the Hudson River from Spuyten Duyvil in order to prove there were no devils in the water. Witnesses claimed to have seen a giant fish that grabbed him by the legs and pulled him beneath the waves. This may be the earliest recorded shark attack in history.

Although NYC has less natural historical affinity with barbecue than, say, Dallas or Kansas City, this art is taken very seriously at the establishment. As far as I am concerned, Fette Sau is one of the best addresses for barbecue anywhere on the planet. The restaurant itself is very well appointed. The eastern wall is entirely covered with a fresco from floor to ceiling, illustrating all of the cuts of a cow, pig and lamb, the only animals that Fette Sau barbecues. The rest of the space is beautifully tiled or decorated in a stylish brown with white painted stripes. A monitor showing a sizzling hearth fire provides a homely coziness.

All the tables are set together, and there is no table service, per se. Shenae keeps an eye on everything with utmost efficiency while people stream in and the line of waiting customers gets longer. All the spectacular meat is displayed and you simply order by weight or according to the number of ribs you desire. In addition, you are offered lovely side dishes that constantly vary. One particular hit is the German potato salad and the chili. Try to come here with a group because if you are only two, you will regret not being able to taste all the delicious smoked meat. Fette Sau is truly the king of the NYC barbecue scene.

# GLASSERIE

eat / drink

11

# GLASSERIE

95 Commercial St. (between Box and Ash St.) - NY 11222
T (718) 389-0640 - www.glasserienyc.com

Open Mon-Fri: lunch 11:30 a.m.-2:30 p.m., Mon-Thu: dinner 5:30 p.m.-11:00 p.m.,
Fri-Sat: dinner 5:30 p.m.-midnight, Sat-Sun: brunch 10:00 a.m.-4:00 p.m., Sun: dinner 5:30 p.m.-11:00 p.m.

"Commercial Street?" the taxi driver asks me. "At Box Street? There is nothing there," he says, "only a few construction sites".

Yellow-fin crudo, strawberries, rhubarb, rose, jalapeno-oil

This dish illustrates the delicateness and subtlety of their cuisine.

Indeed, there are several large construction projects out there to create plenty of living accommodation in Greenpoint, the northern end of Brooklyn.

And indeed, the only taxis that come out here are the ones that drop people off at Glasserie, located in the impressive, former headquarters of Greenpoint Glass Works. This imposing building was built by Christian Dorflinger, a French immigrant from Alsace.

Glasserie belongs to the category of restaurants where you step in and everything seems to fall into place. Owner Sarah Conklin, who is half-Lebanese and grew up in the Middle East, wants her restaurant's kitchen to clearly express her roots and personal preferences.

You don't have to be a bec fin to know how good the food is in this joint. The chef is Eldad Shem Tov, an Israeli whose entire career has been spent with the refined kitchens of the Levant. These influences are clearly there, but in no way domineering. On the contrary, they raise you up into a cloud of flavors; his dishes seem as if they are perfumed by the Middle East, so subtle and fine in flavor they are. The first time I came here, I was totally blown away by the rabbit dish with chickpeas, served with preserved vegetables and a herb salad. This glorious dish of legs of rabbit, confected in duck lard with a slightly smoked flavor, was truly memorable. The saddle was super tender and had the irresistible taste of hawayij, the typical and intense Yemenite spice mix containing ground caraway, saffron, dried onions, cardamom, coriander, black pepper, anise, fennel and ginger, imparting a very characteristic flavor. In the preparation of the other rabbit parts, I thought I also detected urfa biber, which evokes a wonderful smell of sweet plums.

The yellow-fin crudo dish illustrates the delicateness and subtlety of Glasserie's kitchen. Top yellow-fin tuna with strawberries, a hint of rose, refreshing bitter rhubarb, jalapeno oil and, I thought, a whiff of Aleppo pepper. Everything seems to go so naturally here. Sarah Conklin can rest assured that this place is a NY culinary concept in the making.

BREWED IN BROOKLYN
GREENPOINT
BEER & ALE COMPANY
Brouwerij
BROOKLYN · NEW YORK
Dirck the Norseman
GREENPOINT BEER & ALE Co
Gaffel Kolsch
Modern Wit
Mae West
SMASH St XPA
Cheers!

12

# GREENPOINT BEER & ALE CO

7 N. 15th St. (between Gem and Franklin St.) - NY 11222
T (718) 389 2940 - www.greenpointbeer.com

Open Mon-Thu: 5:00 p.m.-midnight, Fri: 2:00 p.m.-2:00 a.m., Sat: noon-2:00 p.m., Sun: noon-midnight

Edward Raven is the owner and driving force of the Lane Brewery on Greenpoint Avenue, Brooklyn's most applauded beer store and café where selected beers were poured.

# Braised pig's knuckle

A wild plan became a reality in the former plastic factory close to the East River waterfront. The space is very impressive and dominated by a big shiny brewery, which is clearly visible through a large window from every corner of the entire establishment. This place is commanded by brewery and beer phenomenon, Chris Prout. Together, they are Greenpoint Beer & Ale Co, the first real brew pub in Brooklyn. The result is a wonderful, gigantic pub with room for live bands and the immense brewing talent of Chris, who can let loose his full creative talent.

The food is ingenious and hearty, and attuned to Chris's beers, not an easy feat. That's why the management decided to keep the food simple but tasty. And as everyone knows – simple is not always easy. There are the perfect ribs, the nostalgic-tasting pork shank and the impressive breast of veal – smoked for eleven hours. Wonderful food that goes perfectly with Chris' assertive beers, such as the Tupelo IPA with a touch of honey added to it, yet remaining refreshing and dry, and Helles Gate Smoked Lager, with a subtle smoky taste. Here you can drink sixteen different beers from the tap, ten of which are brewed on site. Greenpoint Beer & Ale Co is a fantastic bistro by all standards; hanging around here is more of a rule than an exception.

Lucky
Luna
RESTAURANT & BAR
Lucky
Luna
Iced Luna Milk Tea
Michelada $5
2 Tacos for $7.50
Cucumber Salad $7
Lunch 12-3
fetch
RUFF

13

# LUCKY LUNA

167 Nassau Avenue (@Diamond Street) - NY 11222
T (718)383-6038 - www.luckyluna-ny.com

Open Tue-Wed: 5:30 p.m.-10 p.m., Thu: noon-10 p.m., Fri: noon-11 p.m.,
Sat-Sun: brunch noon-5 p.m., Sat: dinner 5:30 p.m.-11:00 p.m., Sun: dinner 5:30 p.m.-10:00 p.m.

In an almost exclusively Polish street in Greenpoint, three friends managed to scrape together $28,000 to kick-start their dream. On a corner that previously housed a pirogi/goulash joint, Lucky Luna became a reality.

# Peking duck confit bao buns, Hoisin mayo & chicharrones

The paths of Howard Jang, Ken Ho and Marisa Cadena hardly crossed previously, but once they met again in NYC, they decided to go for it together. Based on their personal experiences, they decided for a fusion concept, incorporating the Taiwanese and Mexican kitchens, seasoned with a Californian touch. Given the scope and significance of Taiwanese and Mexican cuisines, this is a titanic feat. The dishes are inspired by popular street food from both countries. When I look at it from this perspective and especially when I taste the dishes, I believe that Oaxaca and Taipei have more in common than meets the eye. In any case, both kitchens strive for a balance between sweet and spicy, savory meats and crispy vegetables, presented in bite-sized treats.

Lucky Luna is a breath of fresh air. Due to its tight budget, the focus here is totally on the food and not on a bling-bling interior; that is where their efforts really repay dividends. Howard's kitchen is reduced to a sort of "essence" with extraneous elements discarded, and this approach is rare in a city such as NYC. Moreover, he purposely buys his supplies with a priority for local and highly sustainable products. This really gives him the edge when it comes to flavors.

I admire a chef who prefers to buy items externally if he thinks he cannot outdo them himself – and makes no secret of it. For example, he buys his tortillas from the local Tortilleria Nixtamal in Corona, Queens and the buns from Peking Foods in Bushwick, Brooklyn. On the one hand, there is a subtle fusion of two mega-gastronomical cultures, yet sometimes both cultures are presented neatly alongside one another; that does not make for an easy choice. Just give me everything – that is always my initial reaction. If I taste the finesse and depth of the dishes, I can only conclude that this team has ambitions beyond this soberly decorated, low-profile restaurant.

With the Peking duck confit bao, the chef makes no secret of his admiration for the Korean top chef and entrepreneur, David Chang. Chang put this steamed bun on the world map and since then you see this item crop up in every hip joint, typically locked and fully loaded as the carrier of tons of wonderful ingredients. In all fairness, I have to admit that I find this version more captivating than the last steamed bun I sampled at Momofuku. Howard once again delivers an example of perfect balance and delicateness. In the "reverse" carnitas, the meat is first seared and then braised, rather than the other way around, so it arrives unbelievably juicy. The *nec plus ultra* of neighborhood restaurants!

$ 100 bills
please
CASH ONLY
Toasted Coconut
Turnover
Red Velvet
NOW SERVING
ICE CREAM
DONUT
SANDWICHES
DONUTS
Guaranteed
Fresh Daily,
TO GO
French Toast
All Our Products Are
Made From
100% PURE
VEGETABLE SHORTENI

14

# PETER PAN DONUT AND PASTRY SHOP

727 Manhattan Ave. (Meserole & Norman), Brooklyn - NY 11222
T (718) 389-3676 – www.peterpandonuts.com
Open Mon-Fri: 4:30 a.m.-8:00 p.m., Sat: 5:00 a.m.-8:00 p.m., Sun: 5:30 a.m.-7:00 p.m.

Doughnuts or donuts? You decide how to spell it. Dutch immigrants brought these to the US and they were then called *oliekoecken* or in English, oil cakes.

# Red velvet donut with strawberry ice cream

These fried dough balls made of flour, eggs, butter, herbs, yeast and sometimes dried fruit, rapidly became a popular snack, especially when sprinkled with powdered sugar. Traditionally, the Dutch eat these mainly during the Christmas period, but the history of the donut goes back a long way. They were around in ancient Rome and in the Arab world of the Middle Ages. During the 14th century, they were brought to England, Germany and the Netherlands and from there to the US by pilgrims and immigrants.

An ingenious improvement was conceived - quite by coincidence - by Hanson Gregory. This helmsman was given donut dough by his mother for his journey. During a storm on June 22, 1847, he was at the helm and stuck the donuts on the spokes of the ship's steering wheel, where they stayed put. As it turned out, the hole in the donut made the dough fry more evenly in oil.

The Peter Pan Donut and Pastry Shop is one of the best guardians of the donut tradition. Here, time stands still. The bakers arrive at 1 o'clock in the morning and the first donuts are in the shop at 5 o'clock, warm and smelling great. This store is full of customers throughout the day and the red velvet donuts are usually sold out first.

This National Historic Landmark dates back to the 1950s, but its current owners and guardians of the donut, Christos and Donna Siafakas, purchased the shop in 1993 when Christos was a baker and Donna a waitress in another donut shop in Queens.

The donuts baked here are totally unrelated to the flat and tasteless types produced on an industrial scale, which are sold in every store, gas station and supermarket. Peter Pan donuts have an unforgettable texture and taste and they simply melt in your mouth. This type of businesses should live forever.

GARY

15

# OLMSTED

659 Vanderbilt Ave. (Park & Prospect Pl), Brooklyn - NY 11238
T (718) 552-2610 – www.olmstednyc.com
Open daily: 5:00 p.m.-10:30 p.m.

Olmsted, a small neighborhood restaurant in the heart of Prospect Heights, is currently one of the most extraordinary restaurants in NYC. Most of the ingredients you will enjoy here come straight from the restaurant's back garden, which is very unusual for Brooklyn. The garden is also open for drinks and snacks.

# Carrot Crepe with Littleneck Clams & Sunflowers

The inspiration for this extraordinary project is the fusion of three like-minded souls who met each other at Blue Hill, the ultimate New York example of farm to table cuisine. By the way, Frederick Law Olmsted is the architect who designed Prospect Park. Greg Baxtrom, manager and owner of Olmsted, has worked in the most exciting kitchens in the world: Alinea, Per Se, Atera, Blue Hill at Stone Barns and Lysverket in Norway.

In May 2016, Greg finally felt ready to get his own project off the ground – and it was one to admire. He collaborated with Ian Rothman to create this 50-seat restaurant, which although not vegetarian, focuses on vegetables. His years of experience in many restaurants with various approaches have given him an understanding on how to turn an exciting concept into a success. Ian owns Fairweather Farm in Massachusetts, but attracted attention when he designed an underground garden and 'living' wall for Atera that supply this restaurant with unusual herbs and vegetables. Ian collaborated in that capacity with Blue Hill and Black Tree. When Ian and Greg ran into each other in Atera they instantly knew that they would establish Olmsted based on their passion for and pursuit of sustainable food systems as expressed in a restaurant.

Nothing here is left to chance and that is the only formula that works. You find a top tea list that reveals deep knowledge of tea, a wine list with gems produced by small wineries, which the US if famous for, cocktails made with local ingredients, and so forth.

You walk through the restaurant to reach the back garden. The benches are set up in a U-shape, a bit like the chef's tables in fancy kitchens. The décor is reminiscent of a theater, with the plants and herbs as the main characters: a real pastoral experience in the middle of Brooklyn. There are no tables in the garden, only benches for sitting and nibbling on your snacks, sipping on a cocktail or having a dessert. An occasional quail – raised only for laying eggs, not for eating – comes out of the kitchen to see what's going on outside.

This kind of décor can only deliver perfection on your plate. The dishes are subtle, delicate, spiritual. Some are a study in temperature and texture and a play with cognitive dissonance, just as chef Heston Blumenthal used to do. A lot of deep thought and intelligence went into this cuisine. Paradoxically, Olmsted is currently one of NYC's most ambitious, yet affordable restaurants with a low threshold. Order six or seven dishes to share, perhaps with the exception of the more than fantastic carrot crepe, with its multiple layers, that is simply too good to share. The dish is actually an interpretation of spaghetti vongole, using roots to create a crepe with the colors of a sunflower.

A true remedy for the money-grabbing high-end dinner scene, Olmsted is almost too good to be true.

16

# LEUCA

111 N. 12th St. (Berry & White), Brooklyn - NY 11249
T (718) 581-5900 – www.leuca.com

Open Mon-Fri: 7:00 a.m.-11:00 a.m., 11:30 a.m.-3:00 p.m. and 5:30 p.m.-11:00 p.m.,
Fri till midnight, Sat: 7:00 a.m.-4:00 p.m. and 5:30 p.m.-midnight, Sun: 7:00 a.m.-4:00 p.m. and 5:30 p.m.-11:00 p.m.

Andrew Carmellini is one of the most respected Italian-American chefs in Manhattan. When he managed Cafe Boulud's kitchen, he had a few serious chefs under his wing, such as Rick Torrisi, Mario Carbone and David Chang.

# Fire-Roasted Cabbage, Caesar Flavors

They all looked up to Carmellini. His restaurants are not culinary spectaculars, but they are genuinely delicious and focus on the convivial character of the Italian family kitchen and comfort food.

None of Andrew's other restaurants serve pizza, because this is an entirely different specialty, but in Brooklyn, the pizza capital, there was no way to avoid this. Yet unlike other places, you can't take this pizza home. The elegant restaurant in the William Vale Hotel offers delicious and hardy Italian comfort food, which certainly won't change your life, but will definitely transport you to a typical South Italian town with its lively, chaotic, Italian atmosphere. Leuca, by the way, is a town near Salento in Puglia.

Using fire-roasted cabbage, prepared as a Caesar Salad, Carmellini transforms a vegetable as plain as cabbage into a sex symbol.

On July 4, 1924, when Caesar Cardini made a salad at the request of a customer, he tossed eight ingredients together to create the famous Caesar salad...and the rest is history. Due to the heavy workload on that 4th of July, there were hardly any ingredients left so that the Caesar salad was improvised. When people returned to the eatery and asked specifically for that salad, Caesar realized that he was onto something special. Despite having a home in San Diego, the Cardini family operated a restaurant in Tijuana, Mexico, in order to avoid the Prohibition. To this day, the restaurant, named Caesar's, still serves the original 1924 version of the salad.

Leuca is an ideal spot in Williamsburg for eating great Italian food, especially for people who don't like crossing the bridges to Manhattan.

17

# RAMEN.CO BY KEIZO SHIMAMOTO

13-13 40th Ave, Queens - NY 11101
T (929) 522 0285 - www.ramenshack.com
Open Mon-Fri: 11:00 a.m.-3:00 p.m.

When Keizo Shimamoto traveled around Japan in order to study ramen, he missed NYC very much and had serious yearnings for ... hamburgers.

an insane idea!

# Ramen burger

As a Japanese, this was a totally unexpected experience of culture shock. His brain, driven by homesickness, gave him the impetus for what was to become an insane idea: the Ramen Burger.

With fear in his heart, he presented his idea to the public for the first time in June 2013 at the Smorgasburg festival in Brooklyn. An insane hype was born. The ramen burger was the perfect blend of Japanese and American cultures on the one hand, and two of Keizo's best childhood memories on the other – hamburgers and ramen. The ramen burger in all its varieties is surprising, mischievous, challenging, tasty, confusing. It is naturally not everyone's lot to have an idea, to implement it and see it grow into a phenomenon, as was the case with the ramen burger.

Keizo makes four variations of ramen burgers and they have only one thing in common: there is no bun. The bun is replaced by two perfectly cooked, bun-shaped ramen noodles, held in place by pressing them together and baking them. In between a fantastic Angus beef burger is a bit of arugula, a slice of cheddar, a lovely soy sauce glazing prepared by Keizo and freshly chopped scallions. The other variations are yakitori instead of beef, unraveled beef and tofu.

NYC is now completely subjugated by the ramen burger;, Los Angeles and Hawaii are currently being targeted. There are various new locations in the offing (currently you can only eat a ramen burger at ramen.co and at Smorgasburg) in order to meet the hysterical demand. Recently, BERG'N was opened: a new Beer Garten (899 Bergen Street in Brooklyn, NY 11238) where the ramen burger is always on the menu. Honolulu and LA are next. Stay tuned; it is not inconceivable you will soon see ramen fries!

# BROOKLYN

48th avenue
49th avenue
50th avenue
51st avenue
jackson av
jackson avenue
hunters point ave
skillman av.
51st avenue
borden avenue
2nd street
East River
ash street
commercial street
box street
paidge avenue
dupont street
eagle street
freeman street
green street
huron street
india street
java street
kent street
mcguinness boulevard
manhattan avenue
greenpoint av
greenpoint avenue
franklin str.
west street
milton street
noble street
oak street
calyer street
meserole avenue
norman avenue
humboldt street
newel street
leonard str.
nassau av
nassau avenue
driggs avenue
East River State Park
n 12th street
n 11th street
n 15th street
n 14th street
kent avenue
wythe avenue
n 10th street
n 9th street
n 8th street
n 7th street
n 6th street
n 5th street
n 4th street
n 3rd street
berry street
bedfort av
roebling street
havemeyer street
driggs avenue
McCarren Park
manhattan avenue
brooklyn queens expy
leonard street
metropolitan avenue
n 1st street
grand street
s 1st street
s 2nd street
s 3rd street
s 4th street
hope street
rodney street
lorimer st
metropolitan av
graham av
metropolitan avenue
grand street
grand st
williamsburg bridge
broadway
borinquen place
marcy avenue
s 4th street
keap street
hooper street
hewes street
union avenue
s 8th street
s 9th street
marcy av
division avenue
hewes st
wilson street
broadway
bushwick avenue
montrose av
stagg street
meserole street
johnson avenue
morgan avenue
ingraham street
morgan av
white street
boerum street
seigel street
moore str.
morgan av.
0
500 m
N
2, 11, 13, 15, 16, 24, 19, 20, 25
Brooklyn
East River
manhattan bridge
brooklyn bridge
Brooklyn Bridge Park
york st
high st
clark st
flatbush avenue extension
adam street
nassau street
brooklyn queens expy
borough hall
jay st
myrtle avenue
dekalb ave
dekalb avenue
vanderbilt avenue
nevins st
livingston str.
fulton street
atlantic avenue
court street
bergen st
atlantic avenue
3rd avenue
4th avenue
bergen st
carroll st
union street
3rd street
Brooklyn
clarendon road
avenue d
cortelyou road
ocean parkway
coney island avenue
foster avenue
flatbush avenue
avenue j
bedford avenue
avenue
avenue m
kings highway
ocean parkway
avenue p

## ADDITIONAL EATERIES

18 **EXTRA FANCY**
302 Metropolitan Avenue - NY 11211 (Brooklyn)
T +1 347 422 0939
www.extrafancybklyn.com
▸ **Clam and corn fritters with sriracha ranch dip**

19 **DI FARA PIZZA**
1424 Avenue J (between 14th and 15th Street)
NY 11230 (Brooklyn)
T +1 718 258 136
www.difarany.com
▸ **Calzone**

20 **TACIS BEYTI**
1953-1955 Coney Island Avenue (between Avenue P & Kings Highway) - NY 11223 (Brooklyn)
T +1 718 627 5750
www.tacisbeyti.com
▸ **Kiymali pide**

21 **BROOKLYN GRANGE**
37-18 Northern Boulevard (between 38 and Steinway Street)
NY 11205
T +1 347 670 3660
www.brooklyngrangefarm.com
▸ **Rooftop veggie**

22 **PIES 'N' THIGHS**
166 S Fourth Street (Driggs Avenue) - NY 11211
T +1 347 529 6090
www.piesnthighs.com
▸ **Smoked pork hash and eggs**

23 **NITEHAWK CINEMA**
136 Metropolitan Avenue (between Berry Street and Whyte Avenue) - NY 11249 (Williamsburg, Brooklyn)
T +1 718 384 3980
www.nitehawkcinema.com
▸ **Crab cakes with avocado mayo**

24 **MORGAN'S BARBECUE**
267 Flatbush Avenue (corner of St. Marks & Flatbush)
NY 11217 (Brooklyn)
www.morgansbrooklynbarbecue.com
▸ **16h slow smoked brisket**

25 **CAFÉ TIBET**
1510 Cortelyou Road (Flatbush)
NY 11226
T +1 718 941 2725
▸ **Beef momos**

Joey
RAMONE
S+P

# BRONX

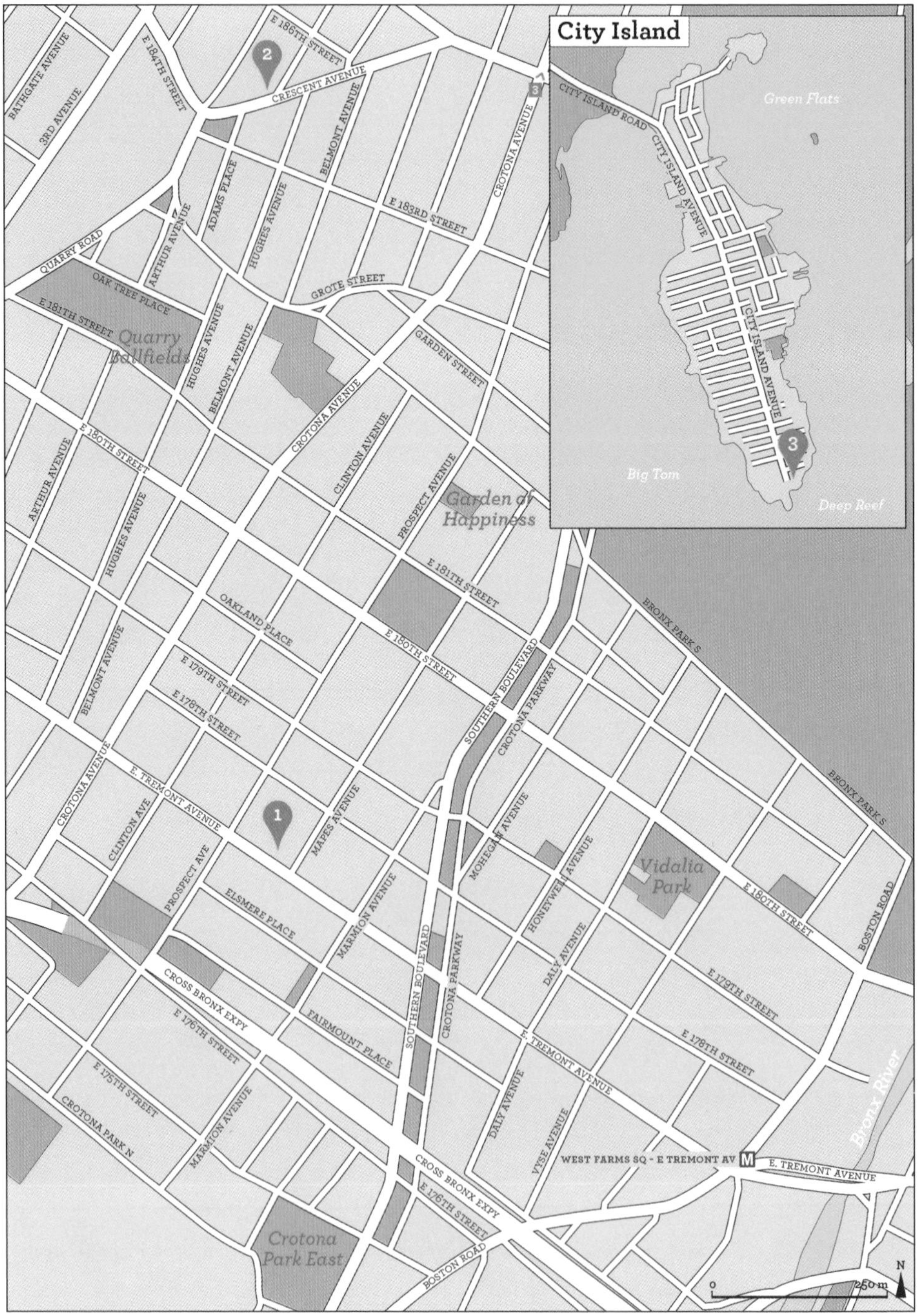

City Island
Green Flats
Big Tom
Deep Reef
City Island Road
City Island Avenue
E 186th Street
E 184th Street
Bathgate Avenue
3rd Avenue
Crescent Avenue
Belmont Avenue
Crotona Avenue
Adams Place
Hughes Avenue
Arthur Avenue
E 183rd Street
Quarry Road
Oak Tree Place
Grote Street
E 181th Street
Quarry Ballfields
Garden Street
E 180th Street
Clinton Avenue
Prospect Avenue
Garden of Happiness
Oakland Place
E 179th Street
E 178th Street
Southern Boulevard
Crotona Parkway
Bronx Park S
E. Tremont Avenue
Clinton Ave
Prospect Ave
Mapes Avenue
Mohegan Avenue
Honeywell Avenue
Vidalia Park
Elsmere Place
Marmion Avenue
Daly Avenue
Boston Road
Cross Bronx Expy
E 176th Street
Fairmount Place
E 175th Street
Crotona Park N
Vyse Avenue
West Farms Sq - E Tremont Av
Bronx River
Crotona Park East
N
0
250 m

## ADDITIONAL EATERIES

1 **EL NUEVO BOHIO LECHONERA**
791 E Tremont Avenue - NY 10460 (Bronx)
T +1 718 294 3905
www.elnuevobohiorestaurant.com
▸ **Roast pork**

2 **ROBERTO'S**
603 Crescent Avenue (Hughes Avenue) - NY 10458
T +1 718 733 9503
www.robertos.roberto089.com
▸ **Pasta e fagioli**

3 **JOHNNY'S FAMOUS REEF RESTAURANT**
2 City Island Avenue (between Rochelle and the ocean)
NY 10464
T +1 718 885 2086
www.johnnysreefrestaurant.com
▸ **Fried seafood and fried fish**

indian accent

1

# INDIAN ACCENT

123 W. 56th St. (between 6th & 7th) - NY 10019
T (212) 842-8070 - www.indianaccent.com
Open Mon-Sat: noon-2:00 p.m. and 5:00 p.m.-10:30 p.m., Sun: 5:00 p.m.-10:30 p.m.

The Indian kitchen is one of the most mysterious kitchens in the world. The complexity of flavors in deep stewing pots is unrivalled. You will find very few restaurants – except a few in India – that can lift these dishes to culinary heights.

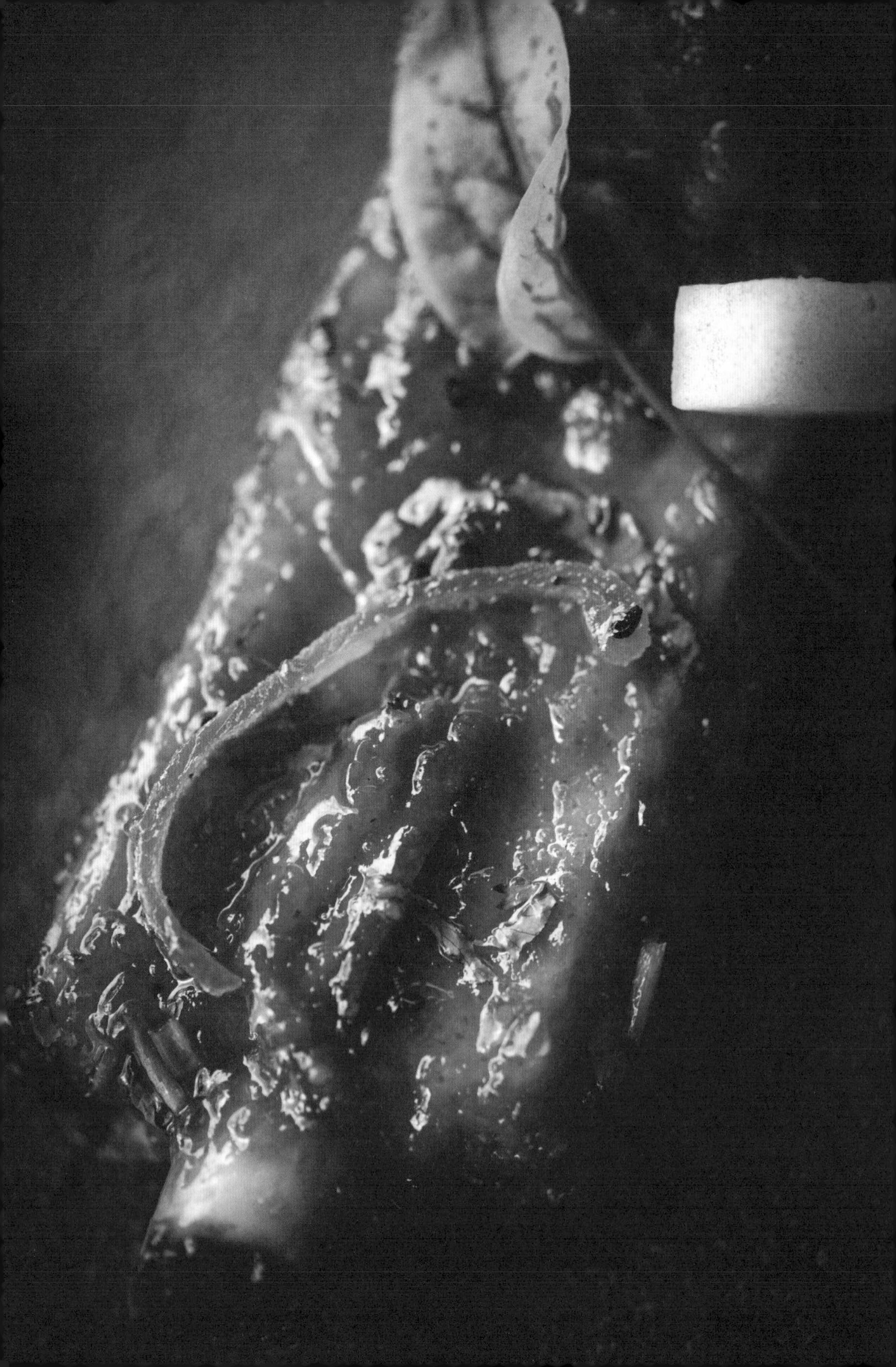

# Sweet pickle ribs, sun-dried mango, onion seeds

In London you will naturally find the famous Rasoi Vineeth Bhatia, and now there is a serious new candidate located in New York City. Manish Mehrota, the chef of Indian Accent, makes it his life's work to reinterpret his nostalgic Indian dishes while being open to international techniques and influences. In this place, progressive ideas seep subtly into Indian dishes without affecting their essence. To achieve this, Manish collaborates closely with the main restaurant in New Delhi. He established this 'mothership' in 2009 when he began in a modest hotel in New Delhi. His international experience in restaurants in Asia and London gave him adequate insight to make the critical New Delhi foodie public curious. They were captured by the quality of the cuisine and, apparently, finally satisfied with their quest to find a place that dislodged itself from the yoke of the traditional Indian kitchen. Manish is considered a liberator of the Indian kitchen.

He allows China, Japan, Mexico and Katz's Deli to seep into his food and that doesn't diminish the experience; it only enhances it. His pastrami-filled kulcha is a statement by any standard and the sweet pickled ribs are out of this world. Let's see if the Manhattan crowd will be as enthusiastic as that in New Delhi.

In any case, I am a great fan and I am always curious to taste the variety of flavors that arrive with the next dish. I would be happy to eat Indian food every day...

# UPTOWN WEST

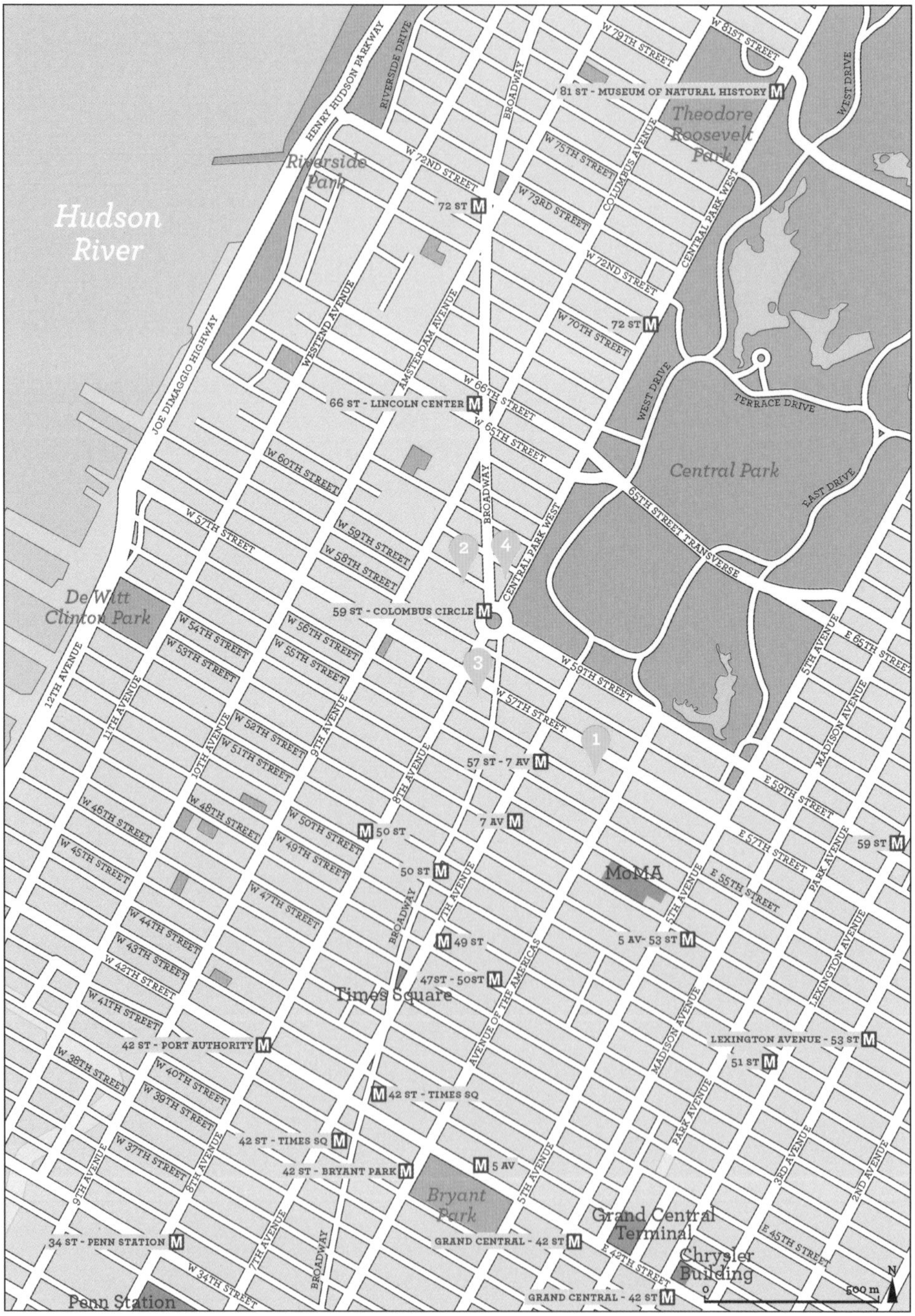
Hudson River
Riverside Park
Theodore Roosevelt Park
Central Park
De Witt Clinton Park
MoMA
Times Square
Bryant Park
Grand Central Terminal
Chrysler Building
Penn Station
81 ST - MUSEUM OF NATURAL HISTORY
72 ST
66 ST - LINCOLN CENTER
59 ST - COLOMBUS CIRCLE
57 ST - 7 AV
7 AV
50 ST
49 ST
47ST - 50ST
5 AV- 53 ST
59 ST
LEXINGTON AVENUE - 53 ST
51 ST
42 ST - PORT AUTHORITY
42 ST - TIMES SQ
42 ST - BRYANT PARK
5 AV
GRAND CENTRAL - 42 ST
34 ST - PENN STATION
1
2
3
4
500 m
N

## ADDITIONAL EATERIES

**ASIATE (MANDARIN ORIENTAL HOTEL)**
80 Columbus Circle (60th Street, 35th floor) - NY 10023
T +1 212 805 8881
www.mandarinoriental.com/newyork/fine-dining/asiate
▸ **Baby carrots with orange blossom**

**PER SE**
Time Warner Centre - 10 Columbus Circle
(4th floor, 60th Street) - NY 10023 (Broadway)
T +1 212 823 9335
www.perseny.com
▸ **9 course tasting menu**

**JEAN-GEORGES**
Trump International Hotel
1 Central Park West (between 60th and 61st Streets) - NY 10023
T +1 212 299 3900
www.jean-georges.com
▸ **Jean Georges Menu**

APT. FOR RENT
MISRAHI
REALTY
(212) 475 • 6660
RGARITA
THE RISING STATES
A

Retail Space
for Lease
Jason Pruger 212.372.2092
Newmark Grubb
Knight Frank
Retail
Lucas Kooyman 212.372.2384
164
164

1

# ROTISSERIE GEORGETTE

14 E. 60th St. (between Madison and 5th Ave.) – NY 10022
T (212) 390-8060 – www.rotisserieg.com

Open Mon: noon-2:30 p.m. and 5:45 p.m.-10:00 p.m., Tue-Fri: noon-2:30 p.m. and 5:45 p.m.-11:00 p.m., Sat: 5:45 p.m.-11:00 p.m., Sun: noon-3:00 p.m. and 5:00 p.m.-9:15 p.m.

Georgette Farkas placed all her culinary trust in top chefs Stefanie Abrams and Francisco Blanco when she started this uptown rotisserie.

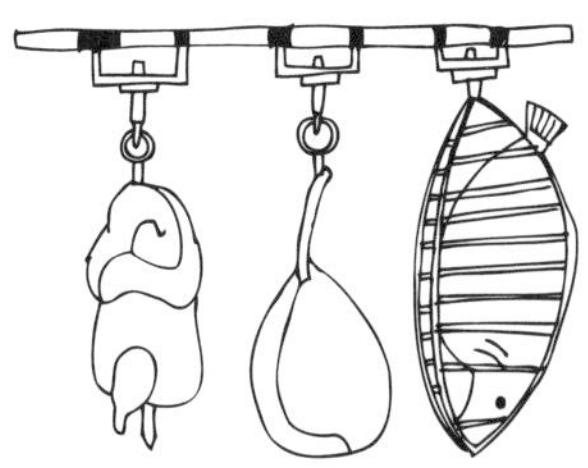

# Poule de luxe

Stefanie originates from Belgium and Francisco is Mexican. Georgette started in the world of restaurants when she was 15. After completing hotel management studies in Switzerland, she went to Monte Carlo to work with Alain Ducasse and later with Daniel Boulud. 17 years later, she was ready to open her own restaurant.

The idea was very simple, yet not so easy to implement. The central concept behind this restaurant is the kitchen theater of Stefanie and Francisco, where the wonderfully spit-roasted delights are professionally prepared.

Whole suckling pig, whole lamb or perhaps a leg of lamb, rabbit, skillfully carved duck, or, of course, the phenomenal roasted chicken. Like many chefs, Stefanie and Francisco prefer to roast whole animals or birds, yet this dynamic duo has complete control of this technique, adding something extra to it; each piece looks tastier than the next. This place serves real food without all the trimmings, yet with lots of passion for artisanship and cooking.

It is great to see chefs who want to please their guests with fantastic flavors and not bluff them with hi-tech cooking techniques or by offering them a taste of food they have never had before. I am actually far more moved by a perfectly grilled chicken leg than a tiny piece of chicken on a fancy plate, surrounded by 15 different mini garnishes. Back to basics has never been so real.

One of the showpieces, the *poule de luxe*, is a full-blooded free-range pedigree chicken, its skin marvelously crispy, with a wonderful mushroom filling; the meat perfectly served with exquisite chicken gravy, wild mushrooms and baked *foie gras*. This is naturally a decadently delicious dish, served for two.

What I have heard about this restaurant is that it has a refreshing lack of creativity. I am not a great fan of one-liners, but this is a very accurate description of Rotisserie Georgette.

# UPTOWN EAST

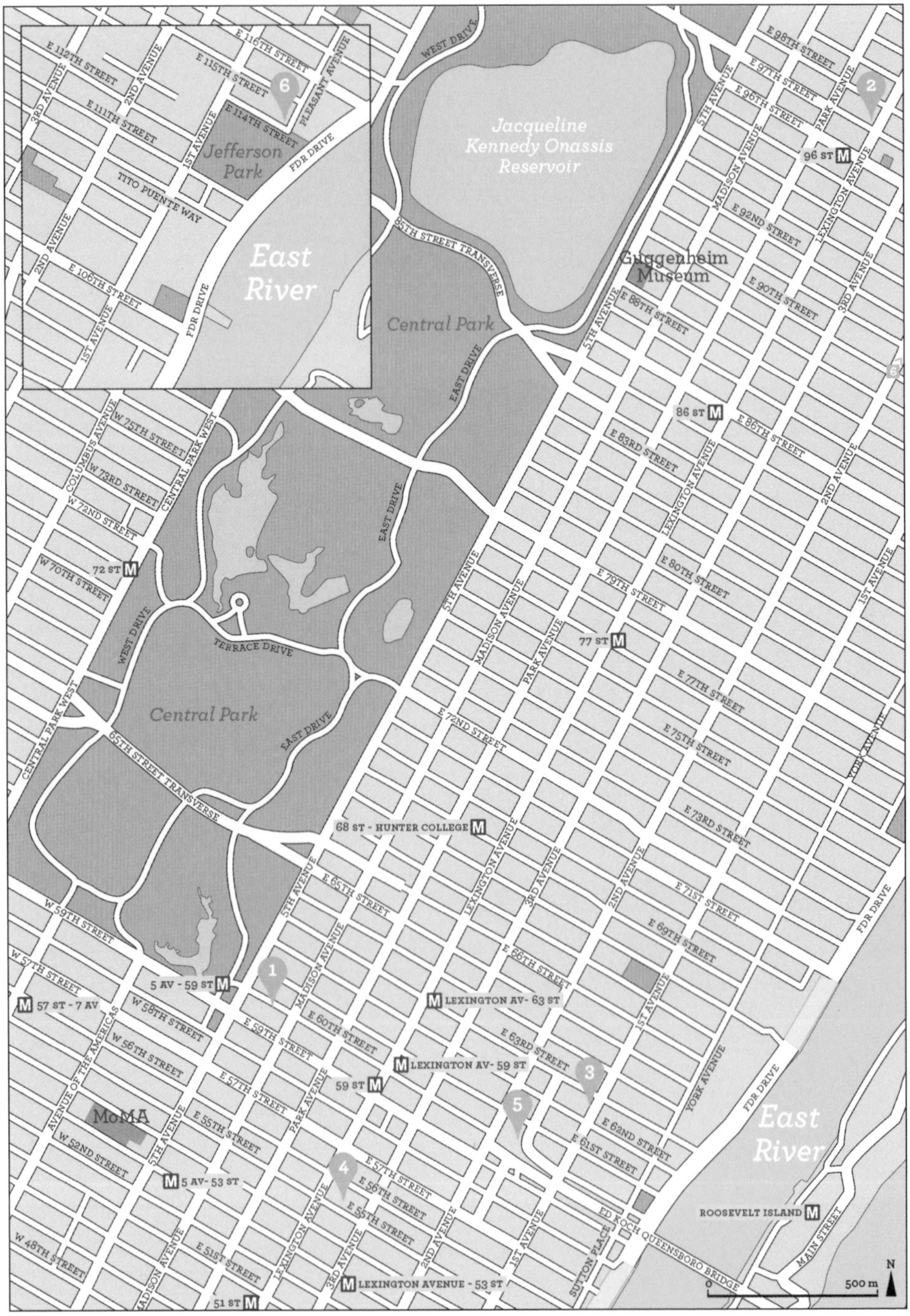
E 116TH STREET
E 115TH STREET
E 114TH STREET
E 112TH STREET
E 111TH STREET
E 106TH STREET
3RD AVENUE
2ND AVENUE
1ST AVENUE
PLEASANT AVENUE
TITO PUENTE WAY
FDR DRIVE
Jefferson Park
East River
WEST DRIVE
Jacqueline Kennedy Onassis Reservoir
85TH STREET TRANSVERSE
Central Park
EAST DRIVE
Guggenheim Museum
E 98TH STREET
E 97TH STREET
E 96TH STREET
96 ST
E 92ND STREET
E 90TH STREET
E 88TH STREET
86 ST
E 86TH STREET
E 83RD STREET
E 80TH STREET
E 79TH STREET
77 ST
E 77TH STREET
E 75TH STREET
E 73RD STREET
E 72ND STREET
E 71ST STREET
E 69TH STREET
E 66TH STREET
E 65TH STREET
E 63RD STREET
E 62ND STREET
E 61ST STREET
E 60TH STREET
E 59TH STREET
E 57TH STREET
E 56TH STREET
E 55TH STREET
E 51ST STREET
5TH AVENUE
MADISON AVENUE
PARK AVENUE
LEXINGTON AVENUE
3RD AVENUE
2ND AVENUE
1ST AVENUE
YORK AVENUE
SUTTON PLACE
FDR DRIVE
W 75TH STREET
W 73RD STREET
W 72ND STREET
W 70TH STREET
72 ST
COLUMBUS AVENUE
CENTRAL PARK WEST
TERRACE DRIVE
65TH STREET TRANSVERSE
68 ST - HUNTER COLLEGE
W 59TH STREET
W 57TH STREET
W 58TH STREET
W 56TH STREET
W 52ND STREET
W 48TH STREET
5 AV - 59 ST
57 ST - 7 AV
AVENUE OF THE AMERICAS
MoMA
5 AV - 53 ST
LEXINGTON AV - 63 ST
LEXINGTON AV - 59 ST
59 ST
LEXINGTON AVENUE - 53 ST
51 ST
ED KOCH QUEENSBORO BRIDGE
ROOSEVELT ISLAND
MAIN STREET
East River
1
2
3
4
5
6
0
500 m
N

## ADDITIONAL EATERIES

2 **FLOCK DINNER**
1504 Lexington Avenue - NY 10029
www.flockdinner.com
▸ **Atypical Eating Event with Corey Cova**

3 **SUSHI SEKI**
1143 First Avenue (between 62 and 63d Street) - NY 10065
T +1 212 371 0238
www.sushiseki.com
▸ **Fried oyster maki**

4 **SHUN LEE PALACE**
155 E 55th Street (between Lexington and 3rd Avenue) - NY 10022
T +1 212 371 8844
www.shunleerestaurants.com
▸ **Peking Duck**

5 **THE JEFFREY**
311 E 60th Street (between 1st and 2d Avenue – Roosevelt island tram station) - NY 10022
T +1 212 355 2337
www.thejeffreynyc.com
▸ **Red beet deviled eggs with House made IPA mustard, chive and dill sriracha**

6 **RAO**
455 E 114th Street (Pleasant Avenue) - NY 10029
T +1 212 722 6709
www.raos.com
▸ **Mozzarella in carozza**

# 1

# NOMAD @THE NOMAD HOTEL

1170 Broadway and 28th St. - NY 10001
T (212) 796-1500 - www.thenomadhotel.com/dining
Open Mon-Thu: 5:30 p.m.-10:30 p.m., Fri-Sat: 5:30 p.m.-11:00 p.m., Sun: 5:30 p.m.-10:00 p.m.

Madison Square Park has always been a public park, as far back as 1686. NoMad (**No**rth of **Mad**ison Square Park) is a neighborhood roughly situated between Chelsea, Murray Hill (where numerous Indian restaurants flourish, creating the recent coinage, "Curry Hill"), Rose Hill and the Flatiron District.

# Chicken

whole-roasted chicken for two, foie gras, black truffle brioche, white asparagus, soft-poached egg

One of the most iconic buildings in the world is no doubt the Flatiron Building, or the Fuller Building, as it was previously known. This unique building, designed in the Beaux-Arts style in the shape of an iron, has stood there splendidly since 1902 and is one of *the* symbols of NYC.

In this neighborhood where Fifth Avenue and Broadway cross, concealed behind a fine-looking Beaux-Arts façade, is the very beautiful NoMad Hotel, recently renovated to its old grandeur by the French designer, Jacques Garcia. It has a real New York feeling, yet at the same time makes playful reference to the European Grand Hotels. Personally, I find it to be of quite the same caliber as the finest Parisian architecture.

However, the real treasure is the fabulous NoMad restaurant, the prodigious offspring of two super-creative people, Daniel Humm and Will Guidara. The identity of the restaurant is built around key words that were used to define the Rolling Stones (loose, alive, genuine, deliberate); these words are inscribed on the kitchen wall not far from a gigantic photo of Mick Jagger on stage.

In the same neighborhood, the duo also operates Eleven Madison Park, a Michelin 3-star treasure, and for a while the gold standard for restaurants in NYC. But rather than rest on their laurels and launch a simple brasserie in this lovely hotel, they opted for a more adventurous approach: They have taken dishes from the Eleven Madison Park kitchen and transformed them into more magnanimous and openly stylish cuisine. While the dishes at Eleven Madison are meticulously prepared, the culinary equivalent of an old Masters painting rendered with a fine paintbrush, the dishes in NoMad are brushed rapidly with a free hand...

Don't be misled; the food here is incredible and one of the best chicken dishes in NYC can be found in this establishment. You order it for two with someone you care deeply about. This majestic dish is stuffed with a pâte made with the most decadent food groups: brioche dough, truffles and foie gras, and presented whole with a bouquet of herbs, a culinary aphrodisiac of the first order. It looks perfect and tastes even better. Keeping the brioche dough under the skin makes the latter wonderfully crispy and the meat unbelievably juicy. It is prepared as two courses by chef Abram Bissell, who serves this masterpiece as unpretentiously as possible, with only a little mashed potato and sometimes some white asparagus. Followed by a fricassee of morel mushrooms and refreshing desserts, this is a complete meal appreciated by true hedonists. It looks like a dish from yesteryear when great chefs used to really value chicken, yet at the same time, it tastes very contemporary.

Rachel Kerswell, the young and talented sommelier from Quebec, has put together an impressive wine list, which I noticed contains a top selection of New York State wines, not routinely found even on Empire State wine lists. A fabulous culinary spot that can easily become a regular habit.

Eisenberg's Sandwich
Continuing Fine Quality Since 1929
212.675.5096
OPEN
EISENBERG'S
WANTED:
Inquire Within!

2

# EISENBERG'S

174 5th Ave. (between 23rd and 22nd St.) - NY 10010
T (212) 675-5096 - www.eisenbergsnyc.com
Open Mon-Fri: 6:30 a.m.-8:00 p.m., Sat: 9:00 a.m.-6:00 p.m., Sun: 9:00 a.m.-5:00 p.m.

Fifth Avenue is one of the most imaginative and inspiring of New York City's arteries. At the point where it crosses Broadway, in the shadow of the monumental Flatiron building, you will find an authentic diner/sandwich shop that looks like it has always been there.

Eisenberg's
Sandwich Shop
Raising New York's Cholesterol Since 1929
HEINZ
57
VARIETIES
HEINZ
TOMATO

# Matzo ball soup

Matzo balls are diveded into the ontological categories of floaters and sinkers.

On the subject of arterial health, "raising NYC's LDL cholesterol since 1929" has been somewhat of a watchword for this establishment. Amidst all the pomp and splendor of 5th Avenue and its adjacent neighborhoods, this authentic jewel has held its own since 1929. That is in no small part due to the many fans and locals who come here regularly to enjoy the many specialties: tuna melt, Reuben and pastrami sandwiches, and of course, matzo ball soup. Aside from the traditional religious significance for Ashkenazi Jews of eating the unleavened bread of their besieged ancestors in Egypt, and in this case eating hearty chicken broth with two matzo balls floating in it, matzo balls have grown into a tasty and widespread comfort food, especially in traditional diners such as Eisenberg's.

According to the dietary laws in the Torah, proper matzo meal can be made of spelt, rye, oatmeal, wheat or barley flour, and mixed with herbs, parsley, a few egg yokes and lightened (or enlightened) with whipped egg whites, one can be served (if the chef is gifted) a matzo ball of sublime texture and appropriate buoyancy. (Matzo balls are divided into the ontological categories of floaters and sinkers.)

This establishment also zealously guards over the genius invention of Louis Auster, namely, the New York Egg Cream; here it is rigorously and meticulously prepared. Auster was a candy-store owner from Brooklyn and he created a kind of forerunner to the milkshake. The etymology has perhaps been lost in translation; the term may originate from the word, 'egg', but more likely from the Yiddish word, '*echt*' (meaning 'real'). What is certain is that the drink became enormously popular and was perfected by Nathan Herman and Jack Witt, both hailing from Crown Heights, also in Brooklyn. Their traditional egg cream was a mixture of chocolate syrup (Fox's U-Bet can still be found commercially), milk and seltzer; the egg is optional, but it does give an extra dimension to the entire mix. Eisenberg's is one of the last places where you can order this fountain drink, since the recipe can never be bottled.

Plenty of tradition and cultural heritage await you at this cozy diner where you are guaranteed to strike up a conversation with one of the many locals who feast there on Reuben or pastrami sandwiches. You won't find many super-cool dudes with beards and tattooed forearms or buns in their hair, but authenticity reigns here. Aida, Eisenberg's very charming hostess, will efficiently help you find your way around this unique world of tastes.

PARK
11

3

# ELEVEN MADISON PARK

11 Madison Avenue - NY 10010
T (212) 889-0905 - www.elevenmadisonpark.com
Open Mon-Thu: 5:30 p.m.-10:00 p.m., Fri-Sun: noon-1:00 p.m. and 5:30 p.m.-10:30 p.m.

Magnificently handsome buildings with distinctive Art Deco influences line the small but extraordinarily beautiful Madison Park. The showpiece is naturally the Fuller Building or the Flatiron Building as it is currently called.

# Tasting menu

*Daniel Humm's work continues to surprise both friends and foes*

One of these beautiful façades, specifically the former Metropolitan Life Building (now the Credit Suisse building), conceals perhaps the most heralded restaurant in NYC: Eleven Madison Park. In 2006, owner Danny Meyer took the brilliant step of bringing chef Daniel Humm on board this ambitious venture. They quickly realized that together they had created a marvelous synergy and would soon be Kings of the City. For their opening in 1998, a wine list was developed with sufficient depth, and of course the setting – the beautiful room – had all the qualities needed to create a memorable restaurant. It was only the food that needed a bit of a boost.

At the age of 25, Daniel Humm of Switzerland had already earned one Michelin star at the Gasthaus Zum Gupf in the Alps. He had made a great impression on Danny Meyer, who was then also the owner of Gramercy Tavern and Union Square Café when they met at Campton Place in San Francisco. The dream team hired Will Guidara as general manager and John Ragan as the wine director. After Daniel Humm and Will Guidara bought Eleven Madison Park from Danny Meyer in 2011, they made the final format switch that made the place what it is today. The restaurant no longer features an à la carte concept, but rather a fantastically daring and surprising tasting menu that tests the imaginative boundaries of your taste buds.

Daniel Humm's work continues to surprise both friends and foes. His carrot tartare is truly amazing and continues to entertain diners: two carrots are ground in a meat grinder attached to your table, then seasoned to taste with various condiments you have selected, accompanied with a quail egg yolk. His creations are personal and with few trimmings; like a stealth bomber, you are blown away by the flavor, balance and depth of the preparations. A truly unique experience. And then there is the magical trick with playing cards at dessert time...

SEAFOOD MARKET
Lobster Place
ESTABLISHED 1974
SUNDAY 10:00AM – 8:00PM
Porgies
Spanish Mackerel
North Carolina
$7.25 lb
Mediterranean
$6.50 lb
WINE
DARJEELING

4

# CHELSEA MARKET

75 9th Ave. (between 15th and 16th St.) - NY 10011
T (212) 652-2121 - www.chelseamarket.com
Open Mon-Sat: 7:00 a.m.-9:00 p.m., Sun: 8:00 a.m.-8:00 p.m.

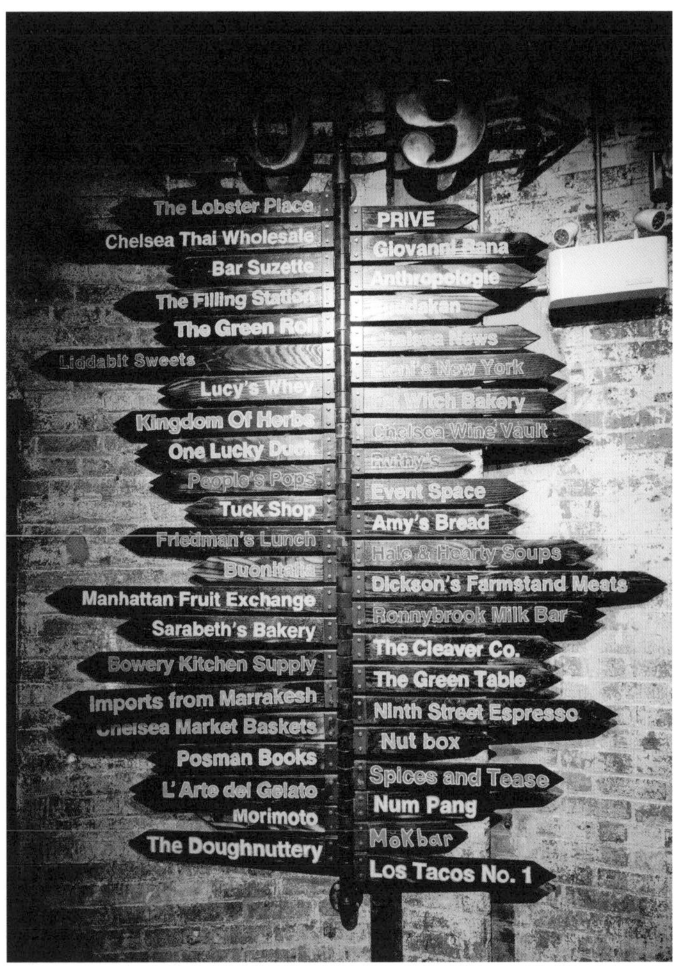


A walk through the old Oreo building, which houses the Chelsea Market, is one of the quickest ways to feel like a New Yorker.

# Local vendors

This building is related to the eponymous cookies; since 1890, all sorts of cookies have been baked in this small factory. From 1990 the building was used for other purposes and offices were set up in the top floors, but what is really interesting is the eclectic mix of food shops, small restaurants and bakeries. The atmosphere here is very homey and everyone walks around enjoying themselves, leisurely chatting with one another. There is lots of eating and it is certainly good eating. The location, by the way, has a historical connection to the production and distribution of food that dates back to the Algonquin Indians and their trade in wild animals and crops. The High Line served the local meat traders and butchers (after all, we are in the middle of the Meatpacking District) before it ultimately became a cookie building. Currently, there are around 35 shops operating in the Chelsea Market and around six million people find their way to this place each year.

The diversity of the offerings is immense and I find it to be a fantastic place for breakfast, brunch or lunch. Stroll along the shops and let yourself be enticed by a homemade donut, a perfectly poached lobster, homemade cold cuts, ice cream, or an espresso. Truly a unique place for just letting go for a while...

CKSON'S
FARMSTAND
MEATS
HotDogs
HOUSE-MADE CHARCUTERIE
PORK
BEEF
Pasture Raised
NO HORMONES
No Antibiotics

5

# DICKSON'S FARMSTAND

75 9th Ave. (in Chelsea Market, between 16th and 15th St.) - NY 10011
T (212) 242-2630 - www.dicksonsfarmstand.com
Open Mon-Sat: 10:00 a.m.-8:30 p.m., Sun: 10:00 a.m.-8:00 p.m.

Whenever I walk through Chelsea Market,
I inevitably get sucked into this top artisanal butchery.

# Handmade artisanal charcuterie

Ted Rosen is a butcher with a real twinkle in his eyes as he tells you about meat and fine cold cuts, and he is even happier when he sees how you enjoy his products.

It is not easy to find artisanal charcuterie or cold cuts in NYC, and seeing that I can't go too long without it, Dickson's is an ideal refueling station. Charcuterie is the drug and I need to score. If you look closely around you, you quickly discover that this is not your run-of-the-mill butchery. It starts with entire animals. The carcasses come in one piece and are entirely chopped up by professional butchers – right in the store where everyone can follow their nimble fingers. The noblest parts are placed on the counter, the less noble parts, but usually the tastiest, are processed in the charcuterie workshop into paté, ham, coppa (cured meat), bacon, pastrami, chorizo sausages, hotdogs, rillettes and blood sausages.

All the meat sold here comes from sustainable, small-scale meat farms. These are small farms that raise traditional breeds and moreover, they don't use any antibiotics or hormones. A four-legged dream. You can come here for delicious cold-cut sandwiches or you can buy the products and eat them at home; there are fantastic cuts of pork, beef or lamb, and fowl. Top address!

morimoto

6

# MORIMOTO

88 10th Ave. (between 15th and 16th St.) - NY 10011
T (212) 989-8883 - www.morimotonyc.com
Open Mon-Fri: noon-2:30 p.m., Mon: 5:30 p.m.-10:00 p.m., Tue-Thu: 5:30 p.m.-11:00 p.m., Fri-Sat: 5:30 p.m.-midnight, Sun: 5:30 p.m.-10:00 p.m.

Iron Chef Masaharu Morimoto is a traditionally trained Japanese chef from Hiroshima, where he formerly owned his own restaurant but sold it in 1985 because he wanted to introduce fusion style cuisine.

only the fattiest part of the tuna is used

# Toro tartare with caviar

After a short stint as a chef at Nobu, it was time for him to open his own restaurants, first in Philadelphia and later here in Chelsea.

The design of this monumental restaurant is stunning, extremely beautiful with lots of room and light, but the spectacular achievement of this Japanese oasis is clearly its top-quality kitchen. At the head of the team is the young and very talented chef, Erik Battes, who certainly infuses the philosophy of the house into all the dishes that are served. I am constantly amazed at how the staff manages to create such a plethora of complex Japanese preparations for such a large number of enthusiastic diners. Here the plates are dressed up with frightful precision.

The kitchen has further developed its own style – thanks to the perceptive diligence of Erik Battes. Although the dishes are still very much Japanese, the kitchen incorporates subtle touches from other gastronomical vernaculars. Japanese dishes are reviewed and restyled, but what is ultimately served comes straight from the mind and heart of a chef who clearly knows what he wants.

One of the things you want to do before you shuffle off this mortal coil is to experience Chef Battes' sublime o-toro tartare, which contains only the fattiest part of the tuna. Nowadays, o-toro, which literally means melting, is considered a superb delicacy, yet even in Japan this has become the case only recently. Before WWII, when fat was considered taboo in Japan, you could go to the Tsukiji fish market and pick up pieces for feeding your cat. Erik Battes prepares his o-toro tartare in an extremely pure traditional fashion, but adds to the lovely plate a variety of seasonings and condiments so that diners can experiment and decide what goes best with the subtle meat of a top o-toro.

KANBUDDAKANBUDDAKANBUDDAK
DAKANBUDDAKANB
UDDAKANBUDDAKANBUDDAKANBUDDAKAN
BUDDAKAN
DAKANBUDDAKANBUDDAKANBUD
KANBUDDAKANBUDDAKANB
UDDAKANBUDDAKANBU
BUDDAKANBUDDAKANBUDDAKAN
DAKANBUDDAKAN
NBUDDAKANBU

7

# BUDDAKAN

75 9th Ave. (@16th St.) - NY 10011
T (212) 989-6699 - www.buddakannyc.com
Open Mon-Tue: 5:30 p.m.-11:00 p.m., Wed-Thu: 5:30 p.m.-midnight, Fri-Sat: 5:00 p.m.-1:00 a.m., Sun: 5:00 p.m.-11:00 p.m.

When I first came here, I didn't get the impression that I was stepping into a restaurant, but rather had been invited to the semi-evacuated property of one or another eccentric Cantonese billionaire, working for SPECTRE.

# Crispy soft shell crab, jicama, watermelon, nuoc mam

I went down the stairs, which led through the central dining area, stately decorated with Chinoiserie wallpaper, and descended into the catacombs, which seem as though they lead to the central safe where it all takes place.

The fact that Buddakan is no ordinary place is noticeable from the moment you enter and find yourself squeezing past NYC's most beautiful people, their faces dimly illuminated by their smartphones, as they call their dates, triangulating on their likely ETAs. My date, the iconic winemaker Egon Müller from the Saar and by coincidence in the city for the NY Wine Experience, had apparently already arrived. The French designer Christian Liaigre, whose design projects include The Market for Jean-Georges Vongerichten in Paris, drew up the plans for a type of Chinese Estate on steroids.

The theme of this mega-XL nightclub/restaurant is the modern Asian kitchen. Most of the time this boils down to disastrous execution, but chef Michael Schulson will make us reconsider. After all, Buddakan is located close to Chinatown, so the inevitable comparison will be made. My experience has taught me that if this is the food you get in a typical Chinatown eatery, you should count yourself lucky.

The choice of dim sum is good and for the most part tastes very authentic. My favorite is a wonderful illustration from the innovative Asian fusion kitchen. Crispy soft shell crabs with a refreshing and crispy salad made from jicama and watermelon in which the sweetness is balanced by the just right quantity of Thai fish sauce. By the way, jicama or yamboon is becoming very popular. This tuber, shaped like a top, is white on the inside, sweet-tasting and deliciously crunchy. The menu changes frequently, but the staff lets you get acquainted with the classical dishes.

8

# ROUGE TOMATE CHELSEA

126 W. 18th St. (between 6th and 7th Ave.) - NY 10011
T (646) 395-3978 - www.rougetomatechelsea.com
Open Tue-Sat: 5:30 p.m.-10:00 p.m.

Is Rouge Tomate a rebel in the New York food scene or is it a visionary restaurant? Whichever, it is certainly unique.

# Mushroom tartare with crispy fingerling potato, roasted garlic and watercress

The main ingredients in this place are plants in all their forms: herbs, seeds, flowers, fruits and vegetables, mostly, but not necessarily combined with meat or fish. The focus here is on your health as well as on sustainability.

Rouge Tomate does seem anti-establishment since it negates the reasons that New Yorkers dine out. No creamy, rich or excessive preparations, but precise, essential dishes with lots of attention to nature.

The chef, Andy Bennett, prepares his dishes with maximum attention to plant-based ingredients. He has long convinced everyone that gourmet eating need not necessarily be unhealthy. Since moving its location from Upper East Side to Chelsea, this restaurant has become more intimate and informal, but it continues to preach its unflagging need to work with local products, to drink only natural wine and above all to exemplify social responsibility. Therefore, its wine list is simply phenomenal and unique. The person responsible for it is the co-owner and one of the most renowned sommeliers in the city, Pascaline Lepeltier. This French master sommelier and lover of Chenin Blanc actually graduated in the discipline of philosophy. She used to be a university lecturer until she decided to follow her heart and devote herself entirely to wine. In 2011, *Wine & Spirits magazine* proclaimed her one of the top five US sommeliers and *Time Out New York* called her a wine prophet. Her list of awards and distinctions is endless. It is more than worthwhile to visit this place, if only for the wine selection. It`s not every day that you are served by one of the most important sommeliers of the nation.

And from a gastronomic perspective, it means healthy eating. What more could you wish for?

Our kitchen
s bigger than
yours.

# CHEF'S TABLE AT BROOKLYN FARE

431 West 37th St, NY 10018, inside Brooklyn Fare market
T (718) 243-0050 – www.brooklynfare.com

Open Tue-Wed: 6:00 p.m. and 6:30 p.m. (counter)/7:00 p.m. and 7:30 p.m. (table)
Open Thu-Sat: 6:00 p.m., 6:30 p.m., 9:30 p.m. and 10:00 p.m. (counter)/7:00 p.m. and 7:30 p.m. (table)

Cesar Ramirez is one of the most honorable chefs that I know. He is modest with no airs and graces and he doesn't participate in TV shows. He prefers to be called a craftsman rather than a chef. I think that he secretly wishes to become a *shokunin*.

# 20+ course tasting menu

This autodidactic cook is of Mexican origin, but was born and raised in Chicago. His greatest mentor is David Bouley, for whom he came to NY to work in his restaurant.

He married a French woman at the age of 19 and used his many visits to France to learn everything about the classical French kitchen and French culinary techniques. The result of his current restaurant is a combination of this knowledge and his intensive visits to Japan.

According to Ramirez, food should speak for itself, without blah blah. Purity and mastery are his mantras.

Moving from Manhattan to Boerum Hill in Brooklyn was a difficult step, but he began a partnership with Moe Issa so that they could start a new restaurant together. Issa grew up here and, after a successful career, dreamed of opening a top delicatessen in this underrated neighborhood full of parking garages. Brooklyn Fare is one of the loveliest gourmet stores I have ever seen, especially because of the almost decadent selection of products that come from everywhere. Together with Cesar, Issa opened the Chef's Table a few doors down and the rest is gastronomical history. Now they are located again in Manhattan, having come full circle.

In addition to the chef, the restaurant is very unique; only 18 chairs at the bar and nothing else. Makes me think of top sushi bars in Japan – that can't be a coincidence. But the real spectacular act is on the plates. Ramirez is at his best when serving fish and crustacean. He flies his sea urchin from Japan and lands it directly on my plate on a rich brioche and a slice of black truffle. His bouillabaisse gives you a peak into the great French classical repertoire; perfectly fried fugu tails land you back in Japan.

Ramirez has a preference for such products, which have always been associated with haute cuisine. His annual expenses for caviar must be enormous. When I see him at work, he always reminds me of a very sincere and wise priest from the East, but once I taste his dishes I am convinced he is one of the best craftsman on the planet.

3
4
5

IVAN RAMEN
EL COLMADO
WINE
Ivan Ramen
slurp shop

The Art of the Slurp

10

# IVAN RAMEN SLURP SHOP

600 11th Ave. (between 44th and 45th St.) - NY 10036
T (212) 582-7942 - www.ivanramen.com/en/ivan-ramen-slurp-shop
Open Sun-Thu: 11:00 a.m.-11:00 p.m., Fri-Sat: 11:00 a.m.-midnight

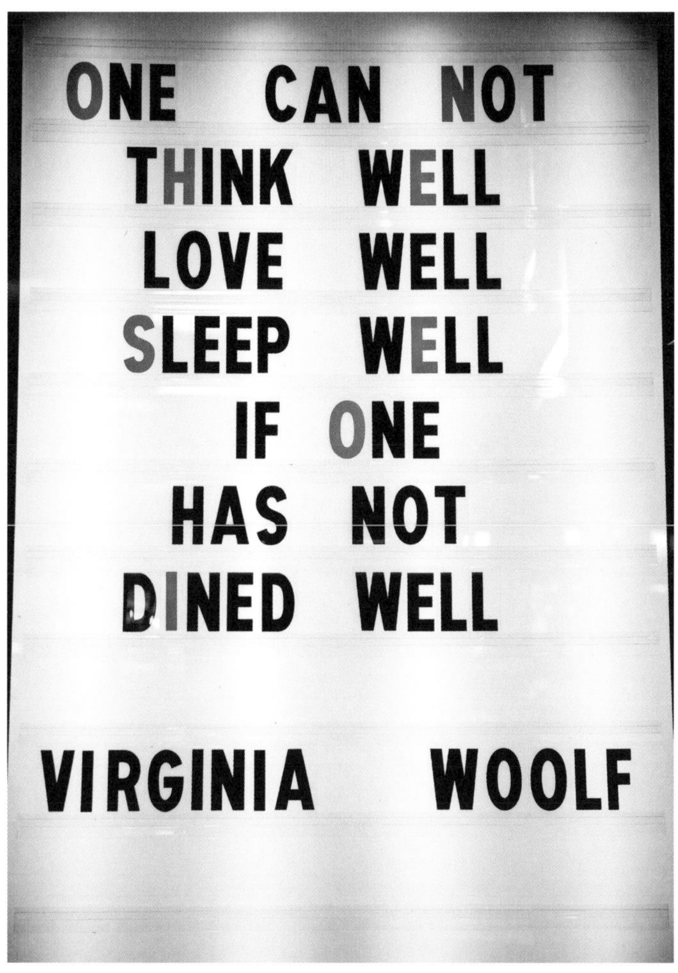


Ivan Ramen is a Japanese ramen noodle bar in the Setagaya quarter in Tokyo; its owner and the driving force behind the bar is chef Ivan Orkin, originally from Syosset, NY.

# Tokyo shio ramen soup

Slurp till you drop!

Ivan lived for many years in Japan and was totally smitten by the complexity of its culinary world. He was especially enchanted by his observation of the refining of the delicate broth used as the basis for Japan's "simple" but wonderful ramen soup. Although he is considered a *gaijin* (foreigner in Japanese), Ivan Orkin dared to open a ramen bar squarely in the lion's den. Initially, the Japanese were very skeptical, but quite rapidly word got around that this *gaijin* really knew his noodles (and broth). A winning rich bouillon and handmade noodles were seemingly all you needed to make great ramen, but it is not as simple as it may seem. This is evidenced by the page-long ramen recipe in his lovely new book, *Love, Obsession and Recipes.*

Fantastic ramen soup is on a strong revival path everywhere, but primarily in NYC where good ramen bars are springing up one after the other. Ivan now has two locations in NYC where people can find his version of the Tokyo shio ramen. The more striking of the two is in Hell's Kitchen, more specifically in the new and spectacular Gotham West Market, which you might sooner call industrial. But don't be fooled by the location; this is by no means an industrial product.

The Tokyo shio ramen is skillfully prepared, based in a hearty rich-layered dashi/chicken broth made with Japanese sea salt, handmade rye noodles and very delicate chashu pork of exceptional depth and complexity. The noodles are cooked to perfection and taste like... I want more. The delicate pork meat melts in your mouth and the creamy yolk provides the finishing touch. A sensation.

Recently, a second location has opened in the Lower East Side at 25 Clinton Street. Slurping is certainly permitted here; in fact, it is very much encouraged.

11

# GABRIEL KREUTHER

41 W. 42nd St. (5th & 6th) - NY 10036
T (212) 257-5826 - www.gknyc.com
Open Mon-Thu: noon-2:00 p.m. and 5:30 p.m.-10:00 p.m., Fri: noon-2:00 p.m. and 5:30 p.m.-10:30 p.m., Sat: 5:30 p.m.-10:30 p.m.

A top location in Midtown Manhattan with a view of the inevitable chess players in Bryant park; you can't possibly wish for more. Gabriel Kreuther was such a rage in NYC as chef of The Modern and must have thought it worthwhile to try his winning formula elsewhere.

# Sturgeon and Sauerkraut Tart

During the first ten years of his career, Gabriel worked in many great Michelin-star restaurants in Germany, France and Switzerland. He then felt ready for a new challenge and began working at Jean-Georges. Once he reached cruising speed, he left Jean-Georges and began his role as Executive Chef of the Atelier in The Ritz-Carlton. He reached his absolute peak at The Modern where he received numerous accolades throughout his nearly decade-long tenure, the high point of which earned him a 2009 James Beard Foundation award for Best Chef of NYC.

In June 2015, Gabriel struck out completely on his own and opened his superb, eponymous restaurant, Gabriel Kreuther. Here, he combines, to his heart's content, his love for New York with his classical French training and his Alsatian heritage. The spirit of Alsace is most prominent in his modern, rural tarte flambée and perhaps in the best liver sausage found within a radius of many miles.

Just like in The Modern, Kreuther does not conceal his classical foundation and stern schooling, both of which work to his advantage. During his brief period as a chef in The Modern he amassed a large number of loyal fans who were absolutely crazy about some of his recipes. It was therefore logical that they followed him to his own restaurant. One of Gabriel's masterpieces is his smoked sturgeon and sauerkraut tart topped with a shiny black American caviar mousseline. This dish could have its own Facebook page with an incredible number of followers.

What is it about his dishes that make them so attractive? They are completely handmade by an enthusiastic and focused brigade that uses techniques which ensure that each dish is both functional and aesthetically pleasing, thus providing real added value.

A true chef, proud of his classical training and his heritage, who has opened an incontestable restaurant.

# MIDTOWN WEST

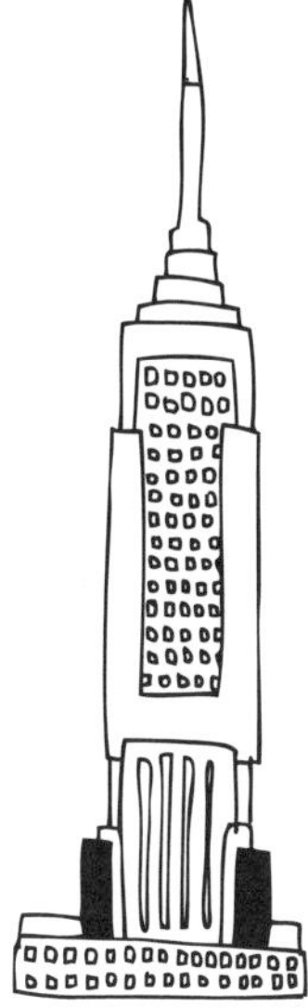

## ADDITIONAL EATERIES

12 **OOTOYA CHELSEA**
8 W 18th Street (between 5th Avenue and 6th Avenue)
NY 10011
T +1 212 255 0018
www.ootoya.us
▸ **Rosu katsu teishoku**

13 **AÑEJO HELL'S KITCHEN**
668 10th Avenue (47th Street) - NY 10036
T +1 212 920 4770
www.anejonyc.com
▸ **Tuna Tlayuda**

14 **CITY SANDWICH**
649 Ninth Avenue - NY 10036
T +1 646 684 3943
www.citysandwichnyc.com
▸ **Portuguese sandwiches**

15 **MAREA**
240 Central Park South (between Broadway and 7th Avenue)
NY 10019
T +1 212 582 5100
www.marea-nyc.com
▸ **Strozzapreti, jumbo crab, sea urchin, basil**

16 **ROBERT'S STEAKHOUSE AT THE PENTHOUSE CLUB**
603 W 45th Street (between 11th and 12th) - NY 10036
T +1 212 245 0002
www.penthouseclubny.com/steakhouse.nxg
▸ **Porterhouse and onion rings**

17 **DAISY MAY'S BBQ USA**
623 11th Avenue (46th Street) - NY 10017
T +1 212 977 1500
www.daisymaysbbq.com
▸ **Pork butt**

18 **GRAMERCY TAVERN**
42 East 20th Street (between Broadway and Park Avenue South) - NY 10003
T +1 212 477 0777
www.gramercytavern.com
▸ **Corn custard, sungold tomatoes and shishito peppers**

19 **PAM REAL THAI**
404 West 49th Street - NY 10019
T +1 212 333 7500
www.pamrealthaifood.com
▸ **Oxtail soup**

1

# UNION SQUARE CAFÉ

101 E. 19th St. (Park) - NY 10003
T (212) 243-4020 - www.unionsquarecafe.com
Open Mon-Thu: 11:45 a.m.-10:00 p.m., Fri: 11:45 a.m.-11:00 p.m., Sat: 10:00 a.m.-11:00 p.m., Sun: 10:00 a.m.-10:00 p.m.

I've always been a great fan and admirer of Union Square Café. When it recently reopened after renovations, I was curious to visit the new Union Square Café. Would it have the same atmosphere? Would I continue to be a fan?

# 19th Street Yellowfin Tuna Burger with tomato, roasted peppers, olive aioli, brioche

The team of architects responsible for the transformation did everything possible to maintain the same atmosphere and they succeeded wonderfully. The eatery that once went by the name of Brownies was rechristened the Union Square Café by Danny Meyer in 1985. Andy Warhol, whose factory was only a block away, was a regular guest. Since that time, it has been inconceivable to talk about the New York food scene without mentioning the Union Square Café. It is a perfect cross between an Italian trattoria, a bistro and an American bar with a grill added for good measure.

Under the ownership of Meyer, Union Square Café has grown into one of the most popular restaurants in Manhattan. The new Union Square Cafe has a little more space: there are 198 seats instead of 152 and if you count the two bars and the spacious loft, you have a more than fantastic restaurant by all standards. The kitchen naturally kept a number of classics, such as the marvelous tuna burger, which after the renovation has been renamed the 19th Street Tuna burger instead of the 16th Street Tuna burger.

Everything in this tremendous restaurant exudes an air of class and friendliness. The morning after one of my visits there, I opened my doggy bag to find a handwritten note from the chef, Carmen Quagliata, expressing her appreciation that I considered her food good enough to take home.

Talented luminary and good friend, Jason Wagner, who previously worked at Fung Tu, was recruited for the ambitious project of updating and maintaining the wine list – which was already quite impressive. Wine has always been an inextricable part of The Union Square Café experience and this is obviously not going to change.

Everything here is just perfect and the customer is truly treated like a king. What appears to be a tourist restaurant is actually an insight into the heart of Manhattan.

BRUT ROSÉ, RAINOLDI '05
VALTELLINA SUPERIORE, SASSELLA, SANDRO FAY '06
BARBARESCO, NUBIOLA, GIORGIO PELISSERO '06
COLIS BRECLEMAE, CANTALUPO '96
SFURSAT, CA' RIZZIERI, RAINOLDI '06
CHIAVENNASCA, CONTI SERTOLI SALIS '08
CAREMA RISERVA, PRODUTTORI NEBBIOLO & CAREMA '05
NEBBIOLO D'ALBA, VALMAGGIORE, SANDRONE '07
GATTINARA, VIGNETO CASTELLE, ANTONIOLO '00
BAROLO, GATTERA,
NEBBIOLO, BRICCO LORELLA, ANTONIOLO '09

2

# MAIALINO

Gramercy Park Hotel, 2 Lexington Ave. (Gramercy Park) - NY 10010
T (212) 777-2410 – www.maialinonyc.com

Open Mon-Fri: 7:30 a.m.-10:00 a.m., noon-2:00 p.m. and 5:30 p.m.-10:00 p.m., Thu-Fri till 10:30 p.m.
Sat-Sun: 10:00 a.m.-2:30 p.m., 5:30 p.m.-10:30 p.m., Sun till 10:00 p.m.

When in Rome, do as Danny Meyer does… Maialino or suckling pig is Danny Meyer's evocation of a trattoria in Rome. The setting for this episode of Dannyland is the Gramercy Park Hotel.

# Four Storey Suckling Pig & Rosemary Potatoes

Everything here exudes Italy. You will be enchanted by the irresistible charm of a *sulami* stand, where they slice excellent Italian charcuterie with great care and even greater love before placing these on blue & white checkered tablecloths.

What makes the Roman kitchen so lovely and special is that the cooks don't feel eternally obligated to smother their pasta dishes with tomato-based sauces and ragù. This is where we find the brilliance of a top chef and entrepreneur such as Meyer. He has the gift to bring out the very best in his chefs within a perfectly clear concept and vision. Nick Anderer, who previously worked at Babbo, was recruited by Meyer to give his Maialino form and taste and to accelerate its operation. Although not a native of Rome, Anderer carries out this role with fervor. Like a seasoned Italian maestro, he creates Roman classics as if they had originated from an Italian grandma's kitchen.

You cannot call a restaurant Maialino without paying tribute to the preparation of the holy pork. An ultimate dish that combines conviviality, sharing and flavor in a single bite is the more than phenomenal suckling pig, magically prepared in the oven. Most of the menu is a tribute to pork, but it also provides an honored place for the less noble meat cuts.

You can't get any closer to Italy in Manhattan than at Maialino.

ATOBOY
ATOBOY
ATOBOY
0/2
A
ATOBOY

## ATOBOY

43 E. 28th St. (Park & Madison) - NY 10016
T (646) 476-7217 – www.atoboynyc.com
Open Mon-Sat: 5:30 p.m.-10:00 p.m., Sun: 5:30 p.m.-9:30 p.m.

Korea or *Uri Nara,* as it is called in Korea, has a very rich culinary culture. The Western name Korea has evolved from Goryeo, the name of the 10th century dynasty.

# Korean fried chicken

The Dutchman Hendrick Hamel (1630-1692) was a shipwrecked sailor who ended up living 13 years in Korea and introduced the spelling of Korea. In the South, the Koreans call their country *Han-Guk* and talk about *Buk Han* if they refer to North Korea and *Joseon* if they refer to their own country. Both however use the name *Uri Nara,* which means our country.

Gastronomically, Korea has a lot to offer, yet you find so few Korean restaurants of noteworthy reputation. If you come across one, it usually serves a bland concoction of *gogigui ofte,* a Korean barbecue, which is a pity, because if something is unknown it is usually unloved.

The eating culture reflects the Korean philosophy on life: striving to achieve yin & yang; warm and cold, mild and hot. An explosion of flavors, aromas and textures; culinary sensations where simplicity reigns.

At Atoboy, they fully understand this. Chef Junghyun Park makes a point of honoring his Korean kitchen and Atoboy was bound to receive Michelin stars. It is an adventurous restaurant with a cool industrial look and it is a real asset to the Flatiron District. Atoboy is a high-level *banchan* restaurant with well-balanced dishes. *Banchan* actually refers to the side dishes that you order with your rice and it is a very popular way of eating in Korea. Here they bestow all the due honors to *banchan.* One of the most popular dishes is *Korean Fried chicken* or *Yangnyeom* which is already a hit in London, New York and Berlin and is also becoming hip in Paris, Amsterdam and Belgium. *Korean fried chicken* means fried twice, just like the Belgians prepare their world-famous French fries. Maximum crispness guaranteed.

For South Koreans, a lavish portion of fried chicken is truly an icon dish, which is washed down with beer or Korean soju. For the older generation, eating chicken is a real treat because during the period when chicken and other meats were scarce, this dish was served only on special occasions. After all, in the 1950s and 1960s there was no chicken available for frying in Korea – it was traditionally cooked with rice and ginseng, a dish called *Samgyetang.* Try this more than fantastic tribute to gastronomic Korea!

Thank You for Shopping With us!
(Please reuse or return to a
Premier
SALAD OIL

# HAANDI

113 Lexington Ave. (between 27th and 28th St.) - NY 10016
T (212) 685-5200 - www.haandiny.com

Open daily: 10:00 a.m.- 4:00 a.m.

If you live in Manhattan without a car and feel like having real Indian cuisine, you may think that you have to hike all the way to Jackson Heights in New Jersey or to Floral Park in Queens. However, there is a sort of mini-Little India close by.

for their chicken tikka I will gladly go the extra mile

# Chicken tikka

The small area of Murray Hill, around 28th Street and Lexington Avenue is very affectionately known as Curry Hill, given the presence of many Indian restaurants there. Here you will find everything that India has to offer, from dosa to Pakistani kebabs, and a very rich and tasty South Indian market.

I am totally addicted to chicken prepared in any conceivable way. Just as I find that the Japanese unagi or kabayaki is the best eel dish in the world, I think that by far the best and most intriguing chicken dish is chicken tikka. The scent, the look, and of course the taste cannot be compared to any other prepared chicken that I know. Chicken tandoori is inextricably associated with India, yet this complex taste explosion originated elsewhere, namely in the Persian Mughal Empire that ruled North India between approximately 1526 and 1757. The rulers were direct descendants of Genghis Khan. The influence of this kingdom was immense; approximately 150 million people were already living in the area at that time.

The dominant cuisine was named after the Muslim Mughlai Empire, operating in the Iranian Kashmir and Punjab regions. Tandoori chicken became popular mainly among the Muslim population at the time when the Mughal Empire fell apart.

The dish found its way into the hearts of North Indians and Pakistanis, and straight into my heart, too. A cut chicken thigh is marinated in yoghurt, lime or lemon juice, along with a mixture of fresh herbs and spices, and is magically transformed by its tenure in the tandoori oven into a piece of emotion. The effect of the yoghurt and lime or lemon juice on the chicken makes the meat very tender. A brief baking time in a traditional, very hot tandoori (900 to 1100 degrees F.) is enough to produce a fire-red chicken thigh that will always give you a different perspective on chicken.

Ali, the very friendly owner of Haandi, keeps a firm hand on the business. I first went into the restaurant because I saw many Indian taxi chauffeurs sitting there enjoying their food. For many North Indian chauffeurs, this is an essential part of their day, just like filling their automobiles with gas. What an amazing discovery! Apart from the buffet, you can also order a large variety of specialties à la carte from the kitchen. For the adventurous diners (temperamental if not direct descendants of Genghis Khan), there is the Magaz masala, split goat-head curry in which the cheeks, tongue and especially the brains are eaten from the skull. Haandi's kebabs are perfectly seasoned and have a nice texture, but for its chicken tikka and tandoori I will gladly go the extra mile.

# SUSHI YASUDA

204 E 43rd St. (between 2nd and 3rd Avenue) - NY 10017
T (212) 972-1001 - www.sushiyasuda.com
Open Mon-Fri: Noon - 2:15 p.m. and 6:00 p.m. - 10:15 p.m., Sat: 6:00 p.m. - 10:15 p.m.

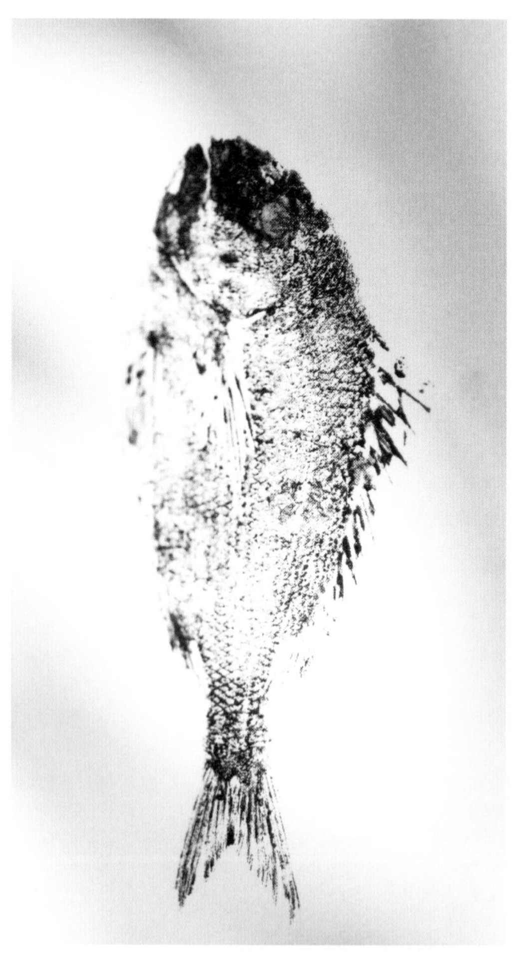

"My life will never be the same," said a good friend of mine after he had his first uni sushi at Yasuda. You can't say I hadn't warned him. He had made his way through countless Japanese eateries, but never outside of Europe, and clearly, he was now playing (or at least spectating) in a different league.

# Uni sushi — sea urchin

Naomichi Yasuda established Sushi Yasuda in 2000 together with Shige Akimoto and Scott Rosenberg and they struck gold from day one. They had the whole proper sushi Gestalt: minimalist, whitewood decor, Japanese hierarchical standards of fanatical quality and precision in the kitchen, fish and seafood flown in from all corners of the globe, a vibrant essential sake list and an immensely driven and talented chef – Yasuda himself.

Many people refuse to believe or simply cannot imagine that it takes ten to fifteen years to master the art of making perfect sushi. Sushi has a very long history that has evolved over time, and one is sometimes privileged to taste the results of these incremental advances of civilized gastronomy. In Japan, if you want to be taken seriously as a sous-chef, you have to practice for many years and only the very best ever attain the status of being *shokunin*, a national treasure, granted only to those who achieve a higher order of excellence through artisanal craftsmanship. I have rarely tasted this level of perfection outside of Japan, but Yasuda hits the mark each time.

Eating sushi must be a complete and sensory experience. Everything must be in place. Stepping into Yasuda means taking a break from the frenetic madness of Midtown East – the restaurant is located just a few steps from Grand Central Station. It feels like you are entering a magical bubble, stepping into a Japanese cocoon. As a welcoming gesture, you are given a glass of water filtered through *binchotan* (rare Japanese charcoal made from centennial oak trees) into a carafe. This establishment is always full, yet the staff retains an eerie level of serenity and poise. These sushi chefs are at one with what they do; they act as a medium for their product, the catalyst that transforms rice and fish into a magical tasting experience. They are capable of extreme focus – think of Japanese photography – which it seems only the Japanese can do with this level of precision. A perfect sushi is a synergistic microcosm that tastes far more complex than its separate ingredients. In this place, every sushi is an experience, a mini-tasting menu in one bite. It begins with the feather-light rice resembling a fluffy cloud, and makes you wonder how the chef succeeds in having the rice grains stick together while constantly keeping their temperature lukewarm.

The choice of super fresh and skillfully handled fish is staggering, making your selection a serious problem. Recommendations are *mirugai* (giant clam), *anago,* Spanish mackerel, *sayori,* cherrystone clam, *hotategai himo* (the spines of sea scallops), and of course, *uni,* the famed, highly erotic sea urchin! The *uni* sushi, or *maki* with *uni* is one of the best bites that you will ever experience in Manhattan.

Initially disorienting, but typical of all top sushi bars, is the absence of soy sauce on the table, because every sushi is made by the master with the quantity of soy sauce that he considers necessary and appropriate. Also typical is the artistically folded finger napkins; after all, you eat sushi with your hands, or better, with your fingers.

Mitsuru Tamura, who worked as the sous-chef for eleven years, took over the task of chef in 2011 when Yasuda went back to Japan to open a sushi bar in Tokyo. Sushi Yasuda is probably the best sushi bar outside of Japan.

# MIDTOWN EAST

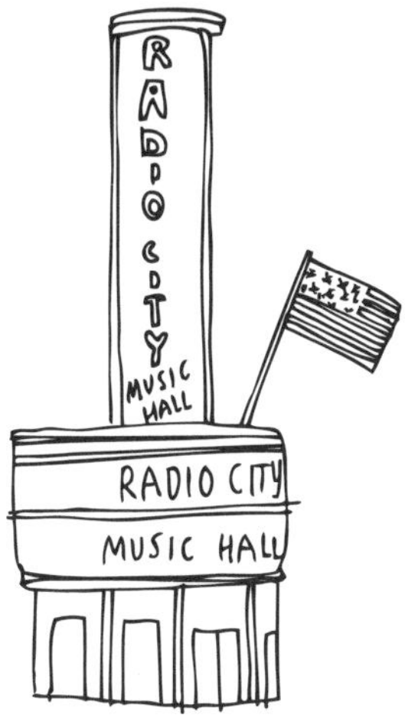


# ADDITIONAL EATERIES

6 **THE GANDER**
15 W 18th Street - NY 10011
T +1 212 229 9500
www.thegandernyc.com
▸ **Beef brisket tots**

7 **KAJITSU**
125 E 39th Street (between Lex and Park) - NY 10016
T +1 212 228 4873
www.kajitsunyc.com
▸ **Shojin inspired omakase**

8 **DHABA**
108 Lexington Avenue (between 27 and 28) - NY 10016
T +1 212 679 1284
www.dhabanyc.com
▸ **Punjab da murgh**

9 **TIFFIN WALLAH**
127 East 28th Street (between Lexington and Park) - NY 10016
T +1 212 685 7301
www.tiffindelivery.us
▸ **South Indian specialties**

10 **AUREOLE**
135 W 42nd St - NY 10036
T +1 212 319 1660
www.charliepalmer.com/aureole_new-york
▸ **Tasting menu**

11 **PENELOPE**
159 Lexington Avenue - NY 10016
T +1 212 481 3800
www.penelopenyc.com
▸ **Chicken pot pie**

12 **NOBU FIFTY SEVEN**
40 West 57th Street (between 5th & 6th Ave) - NY 10019
T +1 212 757 3000
www.noburestaurants.com/fifty-seven
▸ **Black cod with miso**

13 **EMPELLÓN**
510 Madison Avenue
(53rd Street between Madison and 5th) - NY 10022
T +1 212 858 9365
www.empellon.com
▸ **Crab nachos with sea urchin**

Little
CUPCAKE
BAKESHOP
COFFEE & DESSERT
Since 2005

1

# BABBO

110 Waverly Place (between Washington Square West and Avenue of the Americas) - NY 10011
T (212) 777-0303 - www.babbonyc.com

Open Mon: 5:30 p.m.-11:15 p.m., Tue-Sat: 11:30 a.m.-2:00 p.m. and 5:30 p.m.-11:15 p.m., Sun: 5:00 p.m.-10:45 p.m.

The best Italian restaurant in NY
is not located in Little Italy.

aBBO

# Beef cheek ravioli, pigeon liver and black truffles

To enjoy the best Italian food, you have to go to Babbo, the crown of the restaurant empire of the phenomenal chef, author and media star, Mario Batali. He is also an expert in the history and culture of the Italian kitchen, specializing (if one can say that about someone as peripatetic as Mario) in all the regional and local varieties. He is a co-owner of twenty-one restaurants and the author of nine cookbooks.

The grandfather of Molto Mario, as he is sometimes called, left Abruzzo in 1899 to work in the copper mines in Butte, Montana, but later move on to Seattle, where Mario was born in 1960. By now, Batali is a co-owner of various restaurants around the world, but his favorite no doubt is Babbo, which he opened together with Joseph Bastianich.

This place commends the best tradition in Italian hospitality and offers the most exemplary features of Italian cuisine. Their philosophy is simple and straightforward: use only the best local ingredients and serve them as simply as possible. Just as a native of Naples would cook on the Amalfi coast, the cooks at Babbo cook like an Italian on the Mid-Atlantic coast or Hudson Valley. Like most Italian chefs, they love where they live and their kitchen celebrates both their location and their ingredients from the land *and* sea. Babbo is their interpretation of Batali's personal philosophy.

At Babbo you will rarely find your favorite regional classics as you have eaten them in tiny osterias throughout Italy. For me, the menu is a sort of entry ticket into Italian heaven. Batali's versions of Italian *osteria* dishes are sometimes even better that what I remember from Italy. Moreover, the music here is far better than in most Italian restaurants. What always enchants me is the lightness of these seemingly powerful dishes. I only have to think back to the tortellini with goat cheese, sprinkled with dried orange and wild fennel seeds to taste it once again, and this goes just as much for the *brasato al Barolo* (beef braised in Barolo wine), which tastes just slightly better than the version I ate in Brà, at Boccondivino.

Babbo is a phenomenon; the dream of any Italophile and simply a must for every connoisseur of fantastic food and drinks. The wine list by the way is also 100% Italian. Every time I come here, I can think of only one thing: What excuse can I find for coming back here as soon as possible? Forza Mario Batali!

BOULANGERIE

2

# BALTHAZAR

80 Spring Street (@ Crosby Street) - NY 10012
T (212) 965-1414 - www.balthazarny.com
Open Mon-Thu: 7:30 a.m.-midnight, Fri: 7:30 a.m.-1:00 a.m., Sat: 8:00 a.m.-1:00 a.m., Sun: 8:00 a.m.-midnight

One of the most impressive NY restaurants for me is Balthazar.
The place is always packed; that means a kind of cozy chaos.
Yet the dedication and professionalism displayed here in all areas is truly astounding.

# Steak tartare

Shane transforms this seemingly simple dish into a dish of global allure

You feel immediately as if you are in one of the nicest brasseries in Paris, yet served by friendly staff!

It starts with the small bakery next to the restaurant; a small bakery, yet a great one. Just looking through the store window, you are overwhelmed by a feeling of nostalgia and appetite. Feel like having fantastic bread and *viennoiserie*? The brasserie itself is impressive and dynamic, with a menu that changes several times per day. In the evening it seems as if you are looking at a menu in France; the font and colors are selected with the same precision that a choreographer will compose for his or her best dancers. Yup, I am an unconditional fan. There was a time when I used to come here only on Sundays with friends for an extensive brunch or just to read the weekend edition of *The New York Times*, or more plausibly, skim through it, because no one can read it through completely before finishing one's eggs Benedict or sunny-side-up with the homemade blood sausage.

That is why I would like to thank my friends, Olivier and Veerle for making me aware of the marvelous steak tartare. They were both utterly enthusiastic about it and I, of course, became an instant candidate for initiation into this mystical cult. The steak tartare was even tastier than they had described it. Filet americain préparé, known locally as steak tartare, is consumed worldwide. In most places it is briefly marinated beef or horsemeat with as little fat as possible, because raw fat is just not tasty and has a less than pleasant mouth feel.

The version we are familiar with emerged at the beginning of the 20th century in restaurants in Paris in the form of steak à l'américain, made with egg yolk. The dish made culinary history in 1921 when the famous Escoffier included it in his cooking book, *Le Guide Culinaire*. For the purist – there is no inclusion of raw egg yolk – Escoffier was obstinate. In the Larousse Gastronomique of 1938, however, Escoffier's version was adapted and raw egg yolk was insinuated into the preparation.

Shane McBride, the executive chef of this unique restaurant, prepares a version of steak tartare that makes it a foremost reason to come to NYC. The quality of the meat combined with the condiments is a genuine revelation. The brilliance of the seasoning transforms this seemingly simple dish into one of global allure. Because the menu at Balthazar changes several times per day, I always feel like sitting there for hours and ordering something different from each menu. Looks to me like a nice adventure – a day trip to Balthazar, possibly remaining there forever.

KEEP CALM AND CRONUT ON
PLEASE
DOMINIQUE ANSEL BAKERY
DOMINIQUE ANSEL BAKERY
COOKIES
BAKED BY THE HOUR

# DOMINIQUE ANSEL BAKERY

189 Spring St. (between Sullivan and Thompson St.) - NY 10012
T (212) 219-2773 - www.dominiqueansel.com
Mon-Sat: 8:00 a.m.-7:00 p.m., Sun: 9:00 a.m.-7:00 p.m.

Not many bakeries can add revolutionary new items to an already extensive repertoire. To do that and to create perhaps the most febrile buzz the culinary world has experienced in a very long time, in an arena as critical and demanding as NYC, surely suggests that we are talking about an incredibly gifted professional: top French baker, Dominique Ansel.

# Cronut

What is clear is that traveling a lot with an open mind helps one to put daily things in perspective and to see them in a different light. For seven years, Ansel was responsible for the international expansion of the French luxury bakery chain, Fauchon, opening stores in Russia, Egypt and Kuwait. Later on, he had the opportunity to work for six years as executive pastry chef at Daniel, one of the very top restaurants in NYC. At Daniel, Ansel was given great autonomy and this allowed him to greatly develop his skills and creative reach. But he still had more to offer...

At Dominique Ansel Bakery, the eponymous vehicle for the unfettered expression of his creative vision, Ansel had worked for two months on at least ten recipes before he was completely ready to introduce the Cronut™ to the public. This world/historical moment occurred on May 10, 2013 and since then the Cronut has certainly become perhaps the most talked about and copied dessert in the recent history of baking. (Ansel was incidentally proclaimed the "Outstanding Pastry Chef" by the James Beard Foundation in 2014.)

The Cronut is a fusion of the croissant and donut, but it would be an insult to compare this noble creation to a normal croissant or a typical donut. The secret is in the complex proportions of dough utilized and in the fact that it is fried in grape seed oil at a very precise temperature. The Cronut is then carefully rolled in sugar, filled with cream and topped with glaze. The taste changes every month, because Ansel always adapts it to the season. The entire process takes three days and is prepared completely in-house.

The result is a donut that looks like a piece of *viennoiserie*, which you should really eat right away. The inner part is spectacular because of the perfect layers of dough. If you want to cut it (naturally with a serrated knife), it is important not to destroy the layers because they are an essential part of the taste and texture experience.

But how in heaven's name do you get close enough to these delicacies that sometimes fetch up to $100 on the black market? Getting hold of a Cronut is not just a matter of impulse when you have the genial idea of surprising your loved one. You need some serious preparation. Every Monday morning before 11 o'clock, you can place an order via www.cronutpreorder.com for delivery two weeks later! For example, on Monday the 30th of June you can reserve your Cronut for any day during the week between the 14th and 20th of July, with a maximum of five Cronuts per person.

But... the early bird catches the worm. Another way of obtaining a Cronut is to stand in line – like seeking tickets to a Rolling Stones concert – as early as possible before opening hours. The bakery opens at 8:00 or 9:00 a.m. and even at these early hours you will find a long line outside. Yet it's worthwhile; just imagine the look on the face of your dearest when you come home with Cronuts!

A super talent like Ansel of course has much more to offer than just the phenomenal Cronut. His version of French classics such as cannelé and the Paris-Brest (which he calls Paris-NYC) and his blanc-manger are just as delicious. I am totally in love with his madeleines, which are baked when you order them and arrive wonderfully fresh and tasty to your plate. The Cronut is awesome, unbelievably tasty! According to *Time Magazine* this was one of the top inventions of 2013. Believe me, this is really one of the few things that makes waiting in line worthwhile.

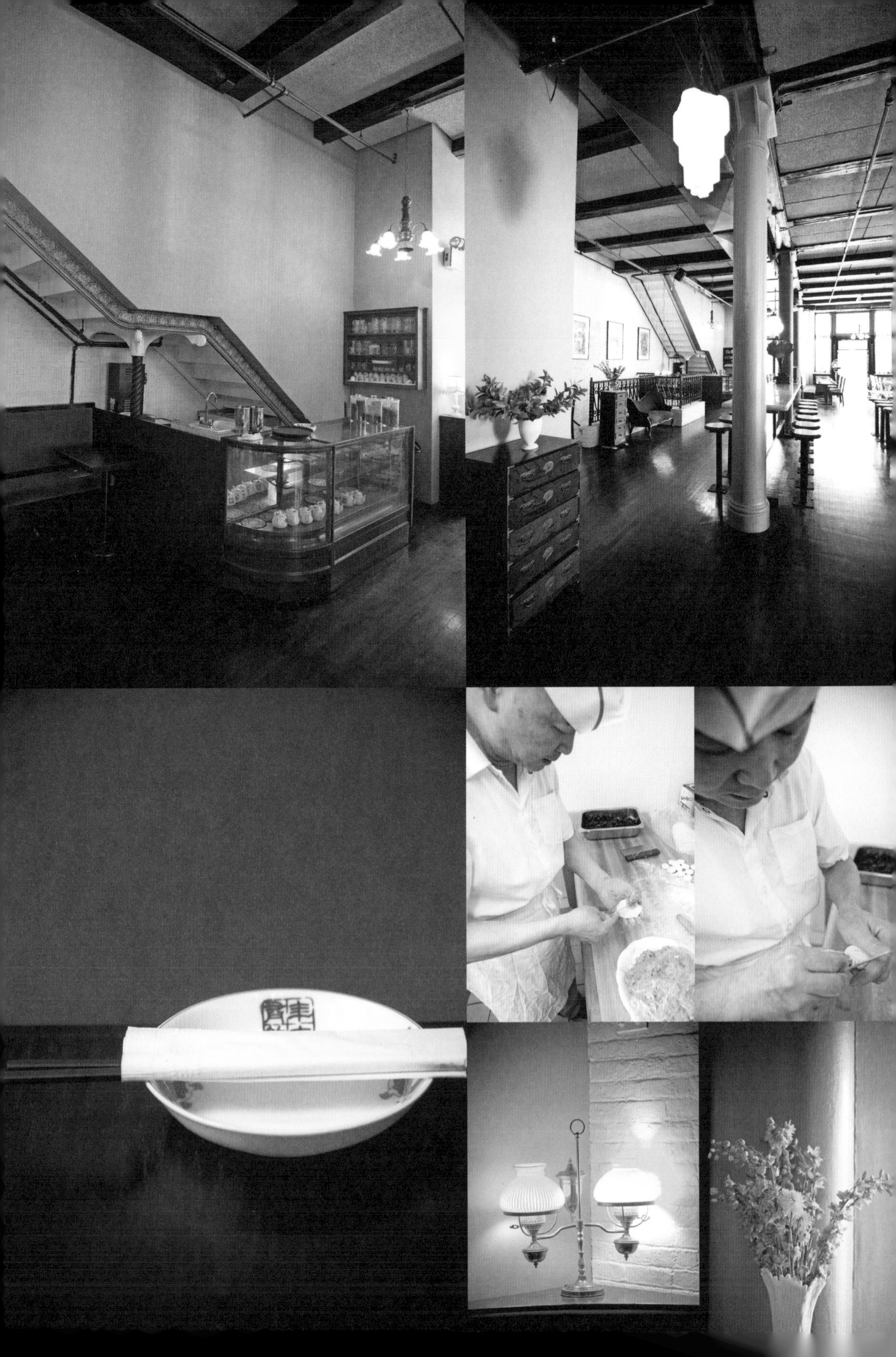

4

# CHINA BLUE

135 Watts St. (or 451 Washington St.) - NY 10013
T (212) 431-0111 - www.chinabluenewyork.com
Open Mon-Wed: 11:30 a.m.-10:30 p.m., Thu-Sat: 11:30 a.m.-11:00 p.m., Sun: 11:30 a.m.-11:30 p.m.

China Blue is one of these restaurants where, after eating, you step outside and think "Everything here is just right!"

finely cut crispy eel, delicately caramelized, sprinkled with sesame seeds

# Crispy eel Wuxi style

It is the brainchild of Yiming Wang, a stylish young woman who has a lot to offer. She not only has a fine taste in food, but she designs her own clothing and apparently does it quite well. In addition, she clearly has a refined sense for interior design, having designed the restaurant herself.

The atmosphere evokes the elegance and distinctness of Shanghai during the period between the two wars. The restaurant radiates classiness and you feel yourself important as soon as you enter. Somehow, this fortunately does not create a particularly onerous feeling of self-consciousness. Antique lamps, used books and old typewriters make for a very special cozy atmosphere. The music, incidence of light, the open space, seem as functional as the space that is used, and of course the fantastic food served here, completes it all.

Chef Li is the salt of the earth and he is very proud of his specialties from Shanghai. Subtlety is the mantra of this kitchen. Also his dim sum chef is a real magician/craftsman. In my opinion, what comes out of this dim sum kitchen has no rival in NY, neither in the realm of authenticity nor in its precision and presentation. A commanding dish that the entire city should taste is the so very typical Xiaolongbao, the ultimate signature Shanghai dumpling and the pumpkin cakes filled with red beans. Choosing a Must Eat here is once again a thankless task, because the number of unforgettable dishes here is countless. For example, I was knocked off my feet by the slow-cooked lion's head meatball, and the eight delicacies in spicy sauce, just to name a few. All the same, I would definitely go for the crispy eel Wuxi style. The finely cut eel is crispy and crunchy and very delicately caramelized, and then sprinkled with roasted sesame seeds. This dish has it all, a complex play of hearty and sweet.

Shanghai cuisine, also known as Hu, is quite popular, closely resembling the cuisine of the surrounding provinces of Jiangsu and Zhejiang. The Chinese sometimes talk about Benbang cuisine when referring to these three. Typical of this cuisine is the use of alcohol, wine, fish and crab. Preserved vegetables and salted meat are often used for flavoring, and sugar and soy sauce are also popular combinations.

LOCANDA VERDE
PASTICCERIA
doughnut 2.
quickbread
muffin
cookie
croissant
scone
coffee cake
breakfast tart 2.
CAFFE
coffee 2
espresso 4
double espresso 6
macchiato 4
cappuccino 4
latte 4
tea 4
24 hour cold brew 3.
"il biscotto primo non é mai perfetto."

# LOCANDA VERDE

377 Greenwich St. (Franklin & Moore) - NY 10013
T (212) 925-3797 - www.locandaverdenyc.com

Open Mon-Fri: 7:00 a.m.-11:00 a.m., 11:30 a.m.-3:00 p.m. and, Mon-Thu: 5:30 p.m.-11:00 p.m., Fri till 11:30 p.m.,
Sat-Sun: 8:00 a.m.-10:00 a.m., 10:00 a.m.-3:00 p.m. and 5:30 p.m.-11:30 p.m., Sun till 11:00 p.m.

A *locanda* is a local Italian inn where you can get a fantastic meal and even spend the night. Although the latter is not actually available here, unless you dine into the early hours of the morning, this green inn is Tribeca's answer to this insanely pleasant, Italian phenomenon.

## Wood-Fired Garlic Chicken for two, Crostini Blue Crab garlic cream, jalapeno, tomato compote

On this busy street corner, it is indeed very Italian. Glorious chaos reigns here morning, noon and night, something only an Italian restaurant would consider acceptable and even enjoyable. It seems that Italians are masters at controlling chaos and succeed in turning it into something cozy and comfortable.

Andrew Carmellini prepares real Italian soul food in this place, using amazing homemade pastas that would make any Italian mamma or *nonna* proud. Carmellini is, of course, not just anybody. For years, he was the chef at Daniel Boulud and he is still somewhat his protegé, which certainly counts as reference. He is a master at classical French preparations, yet works from his roots and heart to create a very attractive and modern perspective on Italian family food. Many people appreciate this cuisine and you certainly witness that. It is surely not the intention here to snap up great culinary prizes, but rather to please guests – whether with an Italian flavored breakfast or a fantastic sausage grinder for lunch, which is after all one of the best sandwiches you will find in NYC. The fantastic chicken for two is a lovely reminder of how simple and delicious Italian food is, especially when you share it. By the way, Locanda Verde is one of the few Italian restaurants where you should try to leave room for dessert. In charge of this is the one and only Karen deMasco, the dessert magician. You can already view her goodies on display at the espresso bar and you will be unable to resist the temptation.

This latest addition to the restaurants owned by Robert de Niro seems more focused and connected to what people really look for in a neighborhood Italian restaurant than his previous attempt. It doesn't get more Italian than this!

JIRO SUSHI
JIRO SUSHI

# 6

# NAKAZAWA SUSHI

23 Commerce St. (between Bedford St. and 7th Ave. South) - NY 10014
T (212) 924-2212 - www.sushinakazawa.com
Open daily: 5:00 p.m.-10:15 p.m.

This is a difficult issue for me: Where can I find the best sushi in NYC? There are two places that ascend above the rest: Yasuda and Nakazawa.

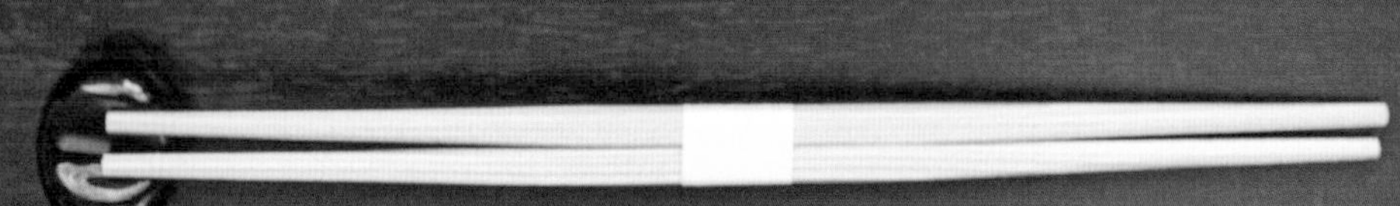

eating here is a magical moment

# Omakase sushi

There is no limit to what television can do! Sometime in August 2012, when Alessandro Borgognone, plopped down on his couch after work in his Italian restaurant and saw a documentary about Jiro Ono (Jiro Dreams of Sushi), the best sushi chef in the world, he was absolutely blown off his rocker by the work ethic and pure craftsmanship of sushi-making. Daisuke Nakazawa was presented several times in this documentary as the most talented and diligent student who had ever worked in the most rigorous restaurant, Sukiyabashi Jiro. That same evening Borgognone contacted Nakazawa – with some help from Google Translate (no less), and in August 2013 Sushi Nakazawa became a fact. Aside from both having clean-shaven heads, Borgognone and Nakazawa don't seem to have much in common, but somehow the two have established a magical bond. Nakazawa is the utmost sophisticated sushi chef, who had to make more than two hundred tamagodashi day after day for his teacher before the latter found them acceptable.

In this quiet tree-lined street in West Village, Nakazawa serves only omakase sushi, a type of tasting menu consisting of 20 sorts of sushi and a temaki. By now, his strict Japanese sushi style has made way for a type of *New York-mae*, a fusion of the best of both worlds.

One hundred minutes of pure heaven is what awaits you if you are one of the lucky people who manage to reserve a table. I had to treat my swollen finger from pressing incessantly on the redial button in order to make a reservation and you would really be crazy not to do it too. Twenty-one courses of sushi from the best waters in the world, freshly flown in, handmade by a genuine, top-master of fish – who additionally has the talent of making a small heap of top-quality rice laid under perfectly cut pieces of fish – feel like a fluffy cloud. Nakazawe is always pleased to show you on his tablet a picture of any fish or seafood that you aren't familiar with. Eating here is a magical moment, as if you have been released from a heavy burden.

LA BONBONNIERE
BURGERS - SNACK BAR — FOUNTAIN

Enjoy
Coca-Cola

FRESH
HOMEMADE 
Bonbonnière 
MEAT LOAF 
PLATE-$10.00
SAND-$8.50
ROAST CHICKEN
Pot & Veg
$10.00
MEAT BALLS
SPAGHETTI
$10.00
MEAT BALL
HERO-$8.50
BOWL OF
CHILI-$6.75
CHILI OVER
RICE-$7.75

7

# LA BONBONNIÈRE

28 8th Ave. (between Jane and W 12th St.) - NY 10014
T (212) 741-9266

Open Mon: 7:00 a.m.-1:00 p.m., Tue: 9:00 a.m.-1:00 p.m., Wed: 9:00 a.m.-noon,
Thu: 8:00 a.m.-1:00 p.m., Fri: 7:00 a.m.-8:00 p.m., Sat-Sun: 7:00 a.m.-4:00 p.m.

A few steps away from super cool Hudson Street you will find La Bonbonnière, a gem of the die-hard breed of diners.

WE SERVE
MENU
HEINZ

# Fluffy Banana pancakes

It even belongs in a rare category: the hole-in-the-wall diner, because it is certainly not big. In spite of its somewhat chic French name, it is a 100% American diner, though it would not snatch too many prizes for its interior design.

The drab brown walls attest to the fact that they have not been painted since NYC became a smoke-free city, and that was easily twenty years ago. However, this does not keep a cluster of fans from swearing by this honky-tonk diner, which is especially popular for breakfast and brunch.

La Bonbonnière does, however, possess a great deal of incredible charm in spite of the Formica counter and plastic chairs. Historically, such places have always attracted celebrities precisely because they can maintain their anonymity in such environments. In La Bonbonnière a celebrity will be less noticeable than at The Standard, for example, because here everyone is busy with themselves and not with their surroundings. From the hall of fame, I did recognize the late James Gandolfini and Ethan Hawke as habitués of the diner. It is really a place that gets to you, and whenever I see the signed CD covers hanging on the wall with titles such as Mike Viola's *The Candy Butchers, Live at La Bonbonnière,* I am endlessly impressed.

I am not actually a great fan of pancakes, but for their fluffy banana pancakes, I make a special exception. They are preternaturally fluffy and light, apparently due to the use of well-beaten buttermilk in the batter. The banana purée in the batter and extra slices of fried banana make this dish a uniquely tasteful experience, even for someone who is not crazy about pancakes.

Ed & Joe Suggest One of Our Grilled Specialties
Events catering Events
Email: events @ redfarmnyc .com
REDFARM

8

# REDFARM

529 Hudson St. (between W. 10th and Charles St.) - NY 10014

Open Mon-Fri: dinner 5:00 p.m.-11:45 p.m., Sat: brunch 11:00 a.m.-2:30 p.m., Sat: dinner 5:00 p.m.-11:45 p.m., Sun till 11:00 p.m.

2170 Broadway (between W. 76th and W 77th St.) - NY 10024

Open Mon-Fri: lunch 11:30 a.m.-3:00 p.m., Mon-Thu: dinner 4:45 p.m.-11:00 p.m., Fri: till 11:45 p.m.,
Sat-Sun: brunch 11:00 a.m.-3:00 p.m., Sat: dinner 4:45 p.m.-11:45 p.m., Sun: till 10:30 p.m.

T (212) 792-9700 - www.redfarmnyc.com

RedFarm is truly custom-made for the super cool Hudson Street. Designer Jun Aizaki knew exactly how to make the owners' wishes come true in this magnificent 1828 townhouse.

# Pac Man shrimp dumplings

It has a pleasant balance between large group tables and small intimate spots where you can sit with one or two people or in small groups.

Joe Ng is a dim sum chef with lots of Kowloon and Hong Kong experience and has a repertoire of more than one thousand of these taste explosions. Ed Schoenfeld has prepared New Yorkers – in an almost missionary approach – for the better Chinese kitchens. This includes the fantastic Shun Lee Palace. Together this is the team of the RedFarm. Ed was immediately convinced of the super talent of Joe Ng, and wanted to give him every opportunity to excel. Joe's aim is to create culinary delights that will even surprise himself.

Joe Ng offers a refreshing look at a number of classics from the Chinese kitchen and he fully comes alive with his very frivolous dim sums. The mushroom and vegetable spring rolls for example look like actual mushrooms and his exquisite ha kau is in the form of a potato tempura Pac chasing Blinky, Pinky, Inky and Clyde. The chicken salad is a sculptural feat and the vegetable salad seems to resemble a vegetable garden.

I truly consider RedFarm one of the very best up-market Chinese restaurants in the city. It really makes the point that one can achieve far better results by making traditional dishes with top-quality ingredients. I believe that RedFarm is the only Chinese restaurant that uses beef from the world-famous butcher, Pat LaFrieda, and I have to dig deep into my memory to come up with a better version of shrimp-stuffed chicken.

In what used to be a Laundromat, RedFarm has recently opened on its ground floor a lovely bar, Decoy, serving Chinese cuisine based on the finger food concept. Joe and Ed are a real dream team and their food definitely belongs in the higher echelons of Chinese food in NYC.

9

# THE SPOTTED PIG

314 W. 11th St. (Greenwich) - NY 10014
T (212) 620-0393 - www.thespottedpig.com
Open Mon-Fri: noon-3:00 p.m. and 5:30 p.m.-2:00 a.m., Sat-Sun: 11:00 a.m.-3:00 p.m. and 5:30 p.m.-2:00 a.m.

This is a very unique spot in the West Village. It is a real British gastropub, as only Fergus Henderson, the founding father of the new British cuisine, could have dreamt up. It is always cozy and busy and everyone wants to be here. It is also a place where you can have a great meal at a reasonable price, which sometimes creates a serious wait because this place only takes walk-ins.

# Chargrilled Burger with Roquefort Cheese & Shoestring Fries

April Bloomfield, a native of Birmingham, is no run-of-the-mill chef. This is evident by both her resumé and the very first bite of whatever dish she puts on the menu. Her experience in The River Café, Bibendum, Mario Batali and naturally Alice Waters got her acquainted with American ingredients. Jamie Oliver advised her to open a bistro-style restaurant in NYC and the rest is history.

A legendary dish in The Spotted Pig is the hamburger. The overall image of this burger is the antithesis of what the average American considers tasty. The roll is homemade and not super-soft, the cheese is Roquefort and not soft American cheese, the burger is 250g and not a 75g flattened piece of misery. This burger sneaks up on you out of nowhere, takes you by surprise and completely smacks your mouth, after which you give in to its sheer delight and passionately eat away with gluttonous bites. This hamburger is what hamburger magic is about...

One of the most moving moments I have ever witnessed on TV was a picture of a scantily-clothed father in a dilapidated bus who had traveled for three days after saving up for an entire year to buy each of his children a cheeseburger at the newly opened McDonalds in Harare. What magic!

Most people think that Ronald McDonald invented the hamburger, but that is far from the truth. Dzjengis and his grandson, Koeblai Khan, traveled with pieces of beef under their horse saddles during their conquests. The constant rubbing made the meat very tender and it turned into ground meat. When Koeblai Khan arrived in Moscow, he mixed eggs and onions into the meat and the first burger was born.

But who was the official inventor of the hamburger? Perhaps it was Otto Kuase, a caterer from Hamburg who, in 1891, made a round roll with fried minced beef, onions, a sauce and a sunny-side up egg, which German seamen introduced to the US. Or maybe it was Delmonico's, a steakhouse in NYC that put hamburger on its menu for the first time in 1826. Or it may be Frank and Charles Menches, who in 1885 at the Erie County Fair in Hamburg, NY, emptied sausages, shaped the meat into round forms and placed it between two slices of bread. There is evidence to believe that the first hamburger sold on a bun can be attributed to Oscar Weber Bilby from Tulsa, Oklahoma, who in 1891, during the 4th of July festivities, sold fried meat balls in between bread slices. The nameplate of Tulsa, Oklahoma, reads: the Real Birthplace of the Hamburger!

Seymour, Wisconsin, became home to a large group of German immigrants and one of them, Charlie Nagreen, aka Hamburger Charlie, sold hamburger steaks at fairs and conventions; minced meat in rolls that passersby ate.

In 1940, a company that would forever change the world's concept of food came up with a great idea: Richard (Dick) and Maurice (Mac) McDonald opened their first restaurant in San Bernardino, California on the corner of 14th and E Streets. 18 years later, they had sold 100 million hamburgers.

Give me the April Bloomfield version anytime, even if you occasionally have to wait in line for half an hour.

# DOWNTOWN WEST

## ADDITIONAL EATERIES

10 **CLAUDETTE**
24 Fifth Avenue (9th Street) - NY 10011
T +1 212 868 2424
www.claudettenyc.com
▸ **Bouillabaise en croûte**

11 **CHEZ SARDINE**
183 West 10th Street - NY 10014
T +1 646 360 3705
www.chezsardine.com
▸ **Foie gras and smoked cheddar grilled cheese sandwich**

12 **DECOY**
529-1/2 Hudson Street (downstairs) - NY 10014
T +1 212 792 9700
www.decoynyc.com
▸ **Peking duck feast**

13 **NOBU DOWNTOWN**
195 Broadway - NY 10007
T +1 212 219 0500
www.noburestaurants.com/downtown
▸ **Spicy uni shooter**

14 **MURRAY'S CHEESE BAR**
264 Bleecker Street (between Morton Street and Leroy Street)
NY 10014
T +1 646 476 8882
www.murrayscheesebar.com
▸ **Seasonal cheesemongers flight**

15 **CORKBUZZ WINE STUDIO**
13 E 13th Street (between University Place and 5th Avenue)
NY 10003
T +1 646 873 6071
www.corkbuzz.com
▸ **Lardo wrapped quail, charred scallion, mint, citrus salad**

16 **CHARLIE BIRD**
5 King Street (6th Avenue) - NY 10012
T +1 212 235 7133
www.charliebirdnyc.com
▸ **Grilled octopus saltimbocca, ceci beans, sage & prosciutto di Parma**

17 **THE DUTCH**
131 Sullivan Street (Prince Street) - NY 10012
T +1 212 677 6200
www.thedutchnyc.com
▸ **Cajun quail, dirty rice shrimp stuffing**

18 **BLUE HILL**
75 Washington Place (between McDougall and 6th)
NY 10011
T +1 212 539 1776
www.bluehillfarm.com/food/blue-hill-new-york
▸ **Daily menu and tasting**

19 **DENINO'S**
524 Port Richmond Avenue (between Hooker Place and Walker Street) - NY 10302 (Staten Island)
T +1 718 442 9401
www.deninos.com
▸ **Garbage pie pizza**

20 **LA PULQUERIA**
11 Doyers St - NY 10013
T +1 212 227 3099
www.pulquerianyc.com
▸ **Chuleta de cerado**

SEXEE
JAKEE
SFGate.com
1996 REMIX STREET LIFE 2015 QUEENSBRIDGE SINGLE
E TO ACC
CIST AME
fascistU

ON
New York
WALLS
DAILY
JESUS
E WAY
TRUTH
LIFE
N 14:6
GOLDLOXE

KATZ'S DELICATESSEN
CATERING
PLATTER ARTISTICALLY DECORATED FOR 18-20 PEOPLE
ROAST TURKEY
ASK FOR OUR SPECIAL BULK PRICES FOR MEAT BOUGHT IN QUANTITY
HORS DOEUVRES
IN BLANKETS
LIVER PUFFS
STUFFED CABBAGE
COLE SLAW
CHOPPED LIVER
FINEST ASSORTMENT COOKIES
BAR MITZVAH WEDDING PARTY CAKES
OUR ONLY STORE
ENJOY!
Catering
FOR ALL
OCCASIONS
SEND A SALAMI TO YOUR BOY IN THE ARMY
RESTROOMS
Heineken
PEPSI
MURPHY'S IRISH AMBER
AT LAST COUNTER
ORDER SANDWICHES HERE
SANDWICH
on RYE
17.45
ORDER SANDWICHES HERE
MURPHY'S
IRISH
AMBER
KATZ'S DELICATESSEN

1

# KATZ'S DELICATESSEN

205 E Houston St. - NY 10002
T (212) 254-2246 - www.katzsdelicatessen.com
Open Sun-Wed: 8:00 a.m.-10:45 p.m., Thu: 8:00 a.m.-2:45 a.m., Fri-Sat: 8:00 a.m.-8:00 a.m.

Pastrami is like a journey in time. The term signifies an age-old method of preserving meat by pickling, drying it slightly, mixing it with various herbs and then slowly smoking and steaming it.

# Pastrami on rye sandwich

Pastrami's origins are not entirely clear. It might have originated in Turkey where it was called pastirma or perhaps in Romania where pastra means 'to store'. We will never be quite sure. What is for certain is that the first pastrami sandwiches in NY emerged during the wave of Jewish immigration from Romania and Bessarabia. In Yiddish it was called pastrome, which evolved into pastrama in English and later, analogous to salami, it became pastrami.

Sussman Volk, a kosher butcher, received a pastrami recipe from a Romanian friend and made the first pastrami sandwich in 1887. This became so popular that his butcher's shop had to make way for a restaurant. In 1888, the Iceland brothers opened a small deli on the corner of Ludlow Street and E. Houston called 'Iceland Brothers'. When they entered a partnership with Willy Katz in 1903, the name was changed to Iceland & Katz. In 1917, it moved to the other side of the street where it is still located to this day. Benny Katz later bought out the Iceland brothers and he is now the one who keeps Katz's cruising along.

Katz's Delicatessen is one of the greatest culinary shrines in NY. It is an institution that lives up to its reputation, time and again. Even though it resembles a football refectory, I can't keep away from this place. It has something magical and enticing for both tourists and locals. The pastrami sandwich is a gastronomical monument, a benchmark, a lodestone for all other pastrami sandwiches in the world. The taste, the texture, the seasoning, all pure perfection, and a sandwich for everyone's bucket list. It should not be forgotten that Meg Ryan experienced her revelatory/orgasmic moment at Katz's in the movie *When Harry Met Sally*. I recommend that you have whatever (no doubt it was the pastrami) she was having.

The Original
YONAH SCHIMMEL
KNISHES
You Don't Have To Be Jewish To Eat A Knish
All Tables Are Reserved For Table Service If You Would Like To Stay ...Please Have A Seat
A Knish A Day Keeps The Doctor Away...
Send Knishes To Your Mother In Florida
FORWARD
The Original
YONAH SCHIMMEL
KNISHES
TABLES FOR WAITER SERVICE
WE DO CATERING FOR ALL OCCASIONS
NO SMOKING
ONE WORLD
ONE TASTE
ONE KNISH
NEW YORK
One World. One Taste. One Knish.

2

# YONAH SCHIMMEL

137 E Houston St. (between 1st and 2nd Ave.) - NY 10002
T (212) 477-2858 - www.yonahschimmelknish.com
Open Sun-Thu: 9 a.m.-7:30 p.m., Fri-Sat: 9 a.m.-11 p.m.

A knish (or knysh) is a traditional snack/meal that was very popular mainly in Eastern Europe.

Potato knish

walk in and have a taste of NYC history

Like many of these types of snacks, they are prepared in different shapes and with a wide variety of fillings. Most knishes are filled with mashed potatoes mixed with minced meat, sauerkraut, onions or cabbage. Kasha, as a filling, was enormously popular in the Jewish Ashkenazi community. They are round, square or rectangular in shape and their size varies depending on whether you eat the knish as a snack or a meal. In cities with a large Jewish population you often still see street vendors selling delicious knishes.

Around 1890, Yonah Schimmel, a Romanian immigrant, began to sell his knishes made from a family recipe. His next logical step was to open a store, and he did that on Houston Street together with his nephew Joseph Berger, becoming the first knish maker in NYC in 1910. Yonah left the business a few years later and Joseph stayed on. The neighborhood has definitely changed in the intervening years; much of the Jewish population has moved out of the Lower East Side, but the little store and the knishes remain unchanged. This authentic neighborhood store is such a NY landmark that we find it in the Woody Allen movie, *Whatever Works*, and in a 1929 painting by Hedgy Pagremanski, which can be viewed in the permanent collection of the Museum of the City of New York. The next time you are strolling past this bakery, walk in and taste a piece of NY history.

Lam Zhou Hand Made Noodle & Dumplin
牛肉拉麵
Beef Soup Noodle
豬肉拉麵
Pork Soup Noodle
羊肉拉麵
Soup Noodle With Lamb
鴨肉墨魚麵
Duck Soup Noodle
水餃　鍋貼
牛尾粉干
Tail Soup With Rice Noodle 22. 6.00
牛杂化
Beef Tripe With thin Rice Noodle 23. 5.50
排骨线面
Steam Pork Soup With Fuzhou Flour Vermicelli 24. 5.50
煎蛋
Fried Egg. 25. 1+/0.5
冰冻汤圆.元宵
Frozen Sweet or Salt rice ball.(50p)26. 12.50
刀削面
House special knife cut soup noodle 27. 7.50.

3

# LAM ZHOU

East Broadway (between Pike and Rutgers St.) - NY 10002
T (212) 566-6933
Open Mon-Sun: 10:30 a.m.- 11:00 p.m.

One of the first things I try to do when I am in Southeast Asia is to have a bowl of hearty noodle soup at one of the countless noodle shops.

# House special hand-cut noodle soup

the perfect bowl of noodle soup exists

This gives me a kind of homey feeling; it is a kind of "Welcome to Asia", disguised as a bowl of soup.

The basic ingredients are broth, noodles, a few fresh vegetables, a bit of fish and/or meat and a few spices. It seems so simple, but the fact that outside of Asia this delicious, steamed noodle soup rarely evokes the same wonderful feeling and flavorful sensation convinces me more and more that we simply do not take this delicacy seriously enough.

This is far from the case at Lam Zhou. The interior is non-existent, as is the décor. Everything here points only to the essential: the food! East Broadway is perhaps not the most aesthetically harmonious street but you should not be misled by the look of a restaurant. Lam Zhou is highly patronized by the Chinese population and a few intimate friends, and it is certainly the kitchen that has merited this attention in virtue of its no-nonsense policy.

The kitchen prepares fresh noodles that are used in an assortment of dishes, mostly in soups or in woks with various garnishes. Believe me, all of these creations are excellent. For the handmade noodles, the portions are chipped off from a thick block of pasta into small, irregular pieces that are processed further. The broth is extremely rich in taste. The handmade noodles offer lots of diversity, considering that they come in a multitude of sizes and thickness. The garnishing of the soups provides a wide variety of genuine taste explosions. A perfect fried egg fully completes the dish. The perfect noodle soup exists!

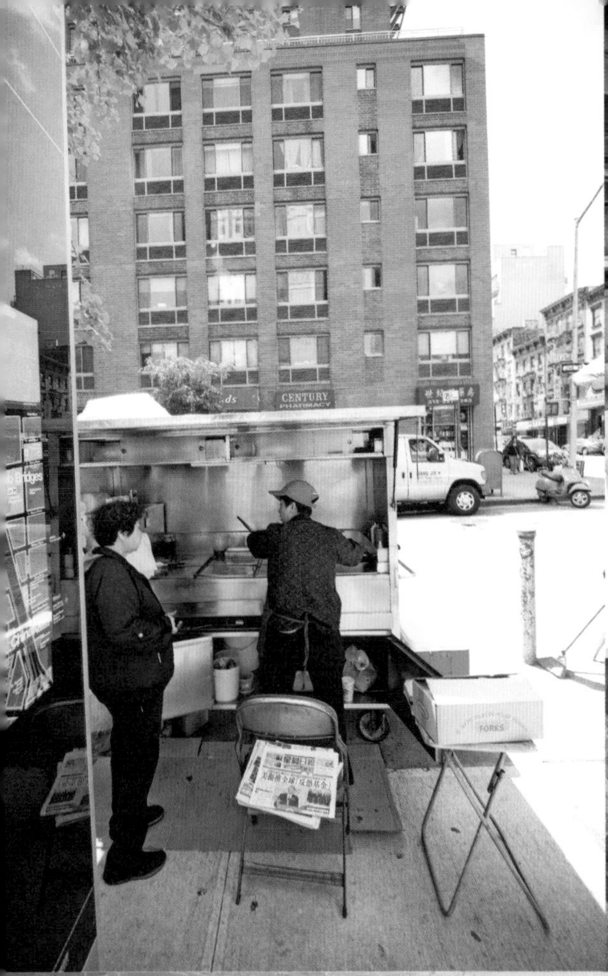

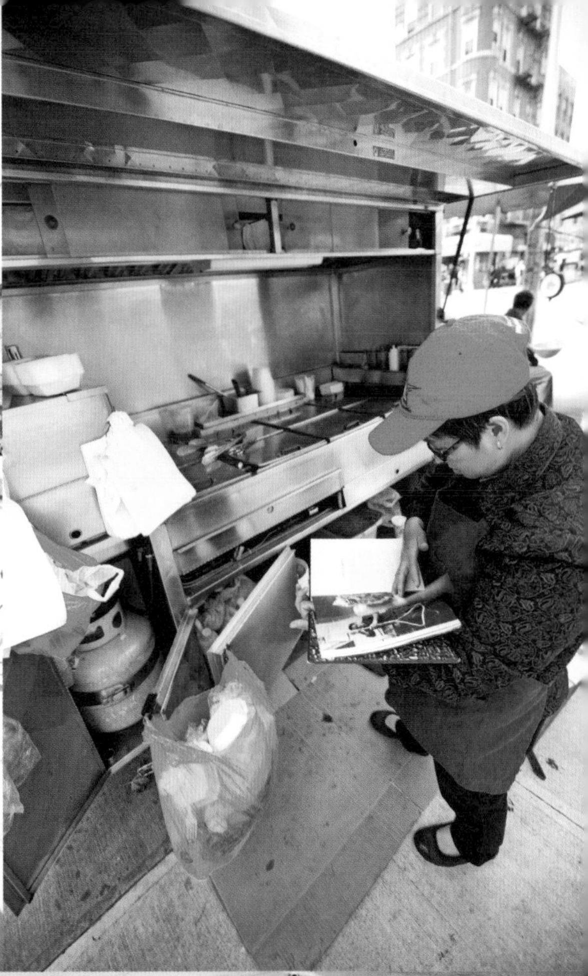

腸粉
Rice Noodles
大L $ 5.00
中M $ 2.50
小S $ 1.75
腸粉魚蛋
Rice Noodles & Fish Balls
大L $ 6.50
中M $ 3.00
小S $ 2.00
茶葉蛋
Tea Eggs
$ 1.25
3只
精制牛肚
Tripe
$ 5.50
腸粉牛肚
Rice Noodles & Tripe
$ 3.25
Extra sauce per order * add 25¢
多醬每一份 加 25¢
爽口魚蛋
Fish Balls
$ 1.00
6粒
正宗咸肉粽
Glutious Rice
$ 1.50
珍珠雞
Glutinous Rice in Lotus Leaf
$ 1.25
炒撈麵
Lo Mein
$ 1.50
炒米粉
Mai Fun
$ 1.50
皮蛋瘦肉粥
$ 2.50
Congee with Minced Pork & Preserved Eggs
$ 1.50

4

# RUTGER STREET FOOD CART

Corner of East Broadway-Rutger St. - NY 10002

Open daily: 6:00 a.m.-4:00 p.m.

There are many small, mobile eating stalls in Chinatown. They all offer their own specialties but to the best of my knowledge only one of them offers tea eggs.

# Tea eggs

the ideal insider snack

Tea eggs are very popular snacks in China and in cities with a large Chinese community. The delicately perfumed, lovely marbled eggs are mostly a feast for the eye, but they are also truly delicious. The idea is actually quite simple. Eggs are hard-boiled and then, with the help of a spoon, randomly cracked into a bowl. The smaller and finer the cracks in the egg, the prettier the end result. After cracking the eggs in the bowl, they are cooked again in a mixture of strong tea, five spices, cinnamon, soy sauce, star anise, fennel seeds, Szechuan peppercorns and cloves. The eggs are heated for another 30 minutes and afterwards remain for a few days in this marinade, obviously having cooled. When you then peel the eggs, the result is exceedingly pretty: the Platonic egg, imbued with heady tea and spice, as well as the very subtle flavor of the marinade. The ideal insider snack.

5

# WILDAIR

142 Orchard St. (Rivington & Allen) - NY 10002
T (646) 964-5624 - www.wildair.nyc

Open Tue-Sat: dinner 6:00 p.m.-11:00 p.m.

Wildair is a little gem in the Lower East Side. It came about due to the success of the Contra restaurant that started to burst at the seams, prompting its owners, Jeremiah Stone and Fabian von Hauske, to open a new business on the same street.

# Beef tartare, cheddar, horseradish, Brazil nuts

Wildair was the name of a famous racehorse that lived here before the Civil War and won many prizes. Nevertheless, there is no horsemeat on the menu! The main theme of Wildair is wine, limited to colorful labels that are made either bio-dynamically or are naturally fermented without any form of intervention. Wildair works with small-scale wine producers who strive for purity and therefore are not well-known among a wider audience. The result is that anyone who enters this eatery is sure to discover a lovely place with even lovelier wines.

Surrounded by wine bottles, the place looks more like a secret society where wine lovers get together to share the latest wine gossip over a bottle of Burgundy. But make no mistake, Wildair serves the very best bar food you can dream of. Nothing here is left to chance. The bread alone (obviously from Contra), with homemade rillettes, is delightful.

The two chefs appear to be unfettered because they cook for a relatively simple wine bar. The beef tartare is an exercise in style for its genre. The perfectly sliced tartar – leaving sufficient bite – mixed with crunchy nuts or buckwheat, spiked with horseradish, and enhanced with smoked cheddar, raises this dish to unrivalled heights, especially when served with the right choice of wine by their wine guru, Jorge Riera.

An eatery that should not be overlooked.

IKINARI STEAK
IKINARI STEAK
NEW YORK
TOTAL NUMBERS
1,184,501
1,184,501
100
You can add extra garnish for $1
Broccoli
Potato
Green Beans
Corn (default)
Onion
Tell our staff upon ordering
You can substitute your default garnish (Corn) with any other vegetables for FREE.
Take Out
Fork
Knife
We Recommend RARE
CUT TO ORDER STATION
Founder of Ikinari Steak
Kunio Ichinose
Tokyo Governor, Yuriko Koike energized herself with Ikinari Steak
来年もお仕置きよ
The article was published in Mainichi Newspapers
Ribeye
weight
Unit Price
144g
482g
9¢
$ Total Price
43$
Steak Sauce
Pepper

6

# IKINARI STEAK EAST VILLAGE

90 E. 10th St. (between 3rd and 4th Ave.) - NY 10003
T (917) 388-3546 – www.ikinaristeakusa.com
Open daily: 11:00 a.m.-11:00 p.m.

Ikinari Steak is the brainchild of Kunio Ichinose, who began this venture in December 2013 and since then has opened more than 100 mini-locations throughout Japan, 60 of which are located in greater Tokyo.

# J-style Rib eye with Garlic Pepper Rice

The idea is simple: serve people top-quality, super-thick juicy steak, but in the most economical way possible. That's why the eatery has mostly standing places. Yes, make no mistake: the idea is to eat your wonderful steak standing up. It is fun, creates lots of interaction and offers New Yorkers a new experience.

When you enter this restaurant, you are directed to an 'eating spot' where the staff takes your order for drinks and side dishes. Every 'eating station' has a number that you take to the chef's butcher corner where you choose from three different cuts: rib-eye, sirloin or filet. You choose the size of your steak, but for a true Ikinari experience of a thick and juicy steak, you should go for at least the 200 g (7.1 oz) or the 300 g (10.6 oz) depending on your favorite cut. Steaks come in all sizes here. They are custom cut and grilled on an open fire. Bleu is the most popular grilling method because the steak is served on a hot cast-iron platter, therefore it further cooks subtly. On the table you will find the superb signature sauce of Ikinari based on a soy sauce so tasty, it absolutely enhances your steak. This is what they call the J-steak experience or the Japanese-style experience. The steaks come from the Aurora Angus beef farm in Illinois and are wet-aged for at least 40 days.

There are only 40 standing spots and 10 seats in this lovely and practical restaurant. Join the customer loyalty program; it's a type of beef mileage card that lets you keep track of how much and what kind of meat you consumed and how this compares to other regular customers. No better place than NYC – the culinary capital of the world – for this nice and dynamic chain to open its first location outside of Japan.

BLACK SEED
170

7

# BLACK SEED BAGELS

170 Elisabeth St. (Kenmare and Spring St.) - NY 10012
www.blackseedbagels.com
Open daily: 7.00 a.m.-4:00 p.m.

For me, the bagel is as inextricably bound up with NYC as the Statue of Liberty. The bagel is nonetheless as old as the street.

## Hand-rolled wood-fired oven poppy seed bagel, homemade cream cheese, beet-cured salmon, radish, herbs

The first time the word "bagel" came up was in 1610 in the municipal by-laws of Krakow, Poland. An interesting anecdote is that in Krakow, any woman who gave birth used to receive a gift of a bagel. The popularity of the bagel grew and in the 16th and 17th centuries it became a part of the daily diet of every Pole. Quite plausible is that the original word derives from *beugal* or *bügel*, due to the irregular shape of the handmade bagels. Bagels were brought to the US by Polish-Jewish immigrants and they quickly gained a strong foothold on these shores. The legendary Bagel Bakers Local 338, dating from the early part of the 20th century, was a tremendous success, creating pride in the craftsmanship required to produce handmade bagels. It was in 1960 that Harry Lender and his son Murray turned the bagel into a national craze when they automated bagel production and began to distribute frozen bagels.

That spelled the demise of the bagel as an artisanal product, but fortunately there were initiatives such as the Black Seed Bagel store. The bagels in this store are made from scratch and waiting in line here also provides a marvelous spectacle. Kate Burr and her team are amazingly motivated, even when the line gets unbearably long. You see all the phases of bagel production occur with precision and dedication, in front of your eyes. Organic flour, salt, water and yeast are kneaded into a hefty dough. The dough is then rolled out into longer sausages and subsequently into the typical ring with the hole-in-the-middle shape of a bagel. Before they are cooked in water, these bagel rings rise for at least 12 hours at 40-50 °F. Once they have cooled down, they are baked in a wood oven at a temperature of 400-570° F. Only respect for these traditional methods will get you a Platonic shiny bagel with the authentic proper texture on the inside.

Since the bagels are made especially for you, you can also choose your filling. The bagels can be filled with sophisticated combinations, resulting in a festive meal. Even while typing these words on my laptop, I can recall the irresistible aroma of fresh bagels. I am totally content whenever I sit on a small bench at the front of this tranquil part of Elisabeth Street while I see and smell the perfect bagel, filled with red beet, lox, homemade cream cheese, fresh radishes and herbs.

Bagels are so popular that on his 2008 Space Shuttle mission, NASA astronaut, Gregory Chamitoff, brought a gift of 18 sesame seed bagels to the astronauts at the International Space Station who had been circling the earth for far too long. Black Seed Bagels change your outlook on bagels forever.

BESSOU
FRITTO MISTO
PRAWNS
SARDINES
CALAMARI
FRIED PARSLEY
BES SOU

8

# BESSOU

5 Bleecker St. (Bowery), East Village - NY 10012
T (212) 228-8502 – www.bessou.nyc

Open Mon-Thu: 5:30 p.m.-11:00 p.m., Fri: 5:30 p.m.-11:30 p.m.,
Sat-Sun: 11:00 a.m.-3:00 p.m. and 5:30 p.m.-11:30 p.m., Sun till 11:00 p.m.

Maiko Kyogoku created this Japanese restaurant mainly because she was homesick, but also because she longed to expand on her family's tradition of sharing a meal. Mealtime in Maiko's home was a way for her mother to communicate with her and her sister and pass on their Japanese tradition and culinary cultural heritage.

# Inaniwa udon

I regret that I have never met Maiko's mother. When I hear Maiko talk of her, or read what she writes about her, I would almost give my right arm to prepare and eat with her the summer cooled inaniwa udon, and in the winter to mash her rice into a pasta to make kiritanpo rice dumplings for one of her stews. Inaniwa udon is a velvety soft noodle dish that originates from the northern prefecture of Akita, and which you can eat warm or cold. It is very typically served as a side dish for tempura that consists of various vegetables which are naturally season based. A dish such as this beautifully reflects the Japanese philosophy: simple yet full of taste due to the right choice of ingredients and perfect control of the cooking technique.

Maiko works a lot with the contemporary artist Murakami with whom she shares her love and respect for Japanese tradition. His desire to share this with the rest of the world is what ultimately pushed her over the threshold to undertake this venture. Therefore, we should largely be grateful to him for Bessou! However, in contrast to the work of Murakami, Maiko is not fully connected to the traditional Japanese forms of representation. Quite the opposite, she is clearly a child of two cultures. On the one hand, she has been exposed to Japanese culture, yet on the other hand, she grew up in the Upper West Side where her father ran a sushi restaurant. She considers herself first and foremost a New Yorker and worked with Murakami primarily in order to learn more about her own background.

Bessou actually means 'second home', a home away from home, and that is no coincidence. The inspiration for the décor came partly from Murakami, but it also greatly reflects the house where she spent much of her childhood. Is New York her *bessou* or is it Japan?

The food at Bessou is Maiko's mature and contemporary view of her youth and her culinary relationship with her mother, combined with the influence of a super metropolis such as New York. The cosmopolitan urban influences obviously make this sort of fusion extra fascinating. As in every Japanese inspired restaurant, it is extremely important to work with seasonal products. Therefore, the menu changes regularly, but not the style or the atmosphere.

At this restaurant cooking is taken very seriously, based on a sensibility that every great artist possesses. No flexing of muscles in this kitchen, but working with flavors that really taste good and leave a lasting impression. I would be happy to call this restaurant my *bessou*.

9

# SAXON & PAROLE

316 Bowery (at Bleecker St.) - NY 10012
T (212) 254-0350 - www.saxonandparole.com
Open Sun-Wed: 6:00 p.m.-10:00 p.m., Thu: 6:00 p.m.-11:00 p.m., Fri-Sat: 5:00 p.m.-11:00 p.m., brunch Sat-Sun: 10:00 a.m.-3:00 p.m.

In case you are wondering, Saxon & Parole is a story of two horses.

# Truffled Portobello Mushroom Mousse with Parole whiskey jelly

Saxon was a magnificent, black racing horse who wore the signature colors of tobacco magnate Pierre Lorillard – cherry red and black. In 1847, this stallion won the Belmont Stakes and overall achieved one of the most impressive lists of accomplishments. Yet, he was overshadowed by the successes of the indefatigable Parole. Born in 1873, this horse, who had more of the appearance of a working horse than an elegant and classy thoroughbred, won nearly all the international races. The British nicknamed him the Yankee Mule because of his atypical look. He became the only American horse to win all the British races. By the time he retired at the age of 12, Parole had won more prizes than any other horse.

The theme of this eatery is grilled meats, aquatic delights and barrel-aged cocktails. On the corner of Bleecker & Bowery, this restaurant was resurrected from the ashes of the Double Crown. Although the bar remained intact, the rest of the restaurant was given a facelift, becoming a more modern brasserie. In the kitchen, Brad Farmerie prepares dishes that are more continental with a very high content of comfort food.

This and the more than fantastic bar ensure that Saxon & Parole is an ideal clubhouse for the East Villagers. The interior is warm and welcoming, lots of bare bricks and Edison style lighting that reflects on the light wood paneling, a typical AvroKo look. This top design company has left its mark on countless successful restaurants in NYC. You have a choice of three dining halls, so you can select your personal atmosphere. For the insiders: the western wall of the second dining hall – the one with leather benches and a marble fireplace – has a hidden door that leads to Madame Geneva, a neighboring speakeasy, a famous watering hole for insiders.

Lots to experience here at Saxon & Parole; a nice place to spend time.

Live GeoDuck Clam
新鲜象拔蚌

10

# ORIENTAL GARDEN

14 Elisabeth St. (between Canal and Bayard St.) - NY 10013
T (212) 619-0085 - www.orientalgardennyc.com
Open daily: 10:00 a.m.-10:30 p.m.

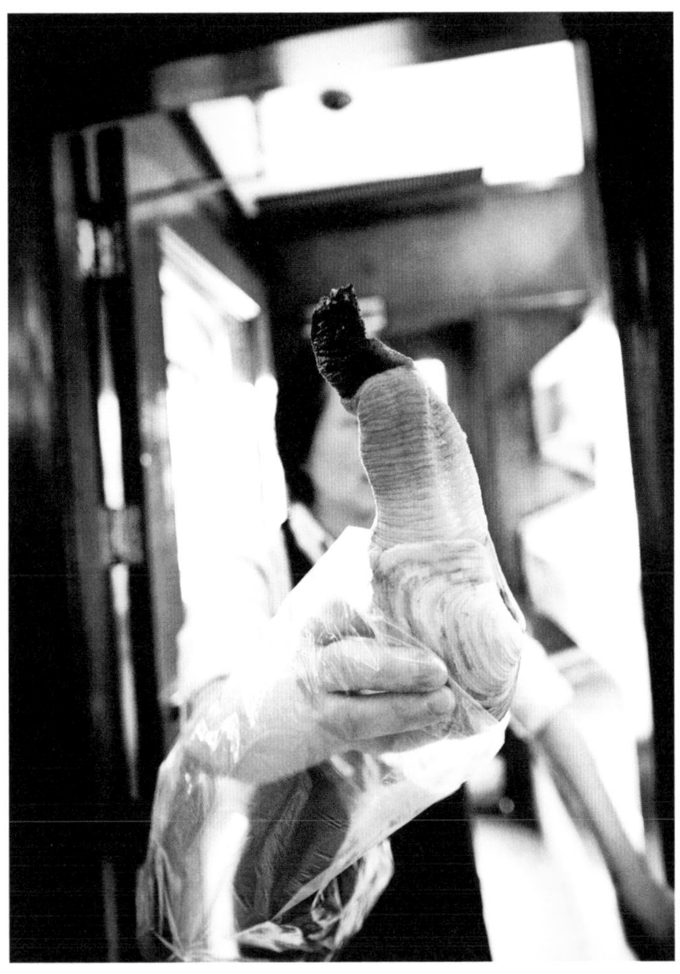

In NYC's vast Chinatown it is not always so easy to separate the wheat from the chaff.

they work genuine magic with live Geoduck

# Raw sliced geoduck

Every place has its specialty and in this restaurant it is most definitely fish and seafood. To make the point clear, this unique Cantonese restaurant features numerous aquariums at its entrance, insuring that all of its delicious offerings are as fresh as they can be.

Another special feature of the restaurant is the separate cooler where the more unique and currently available seafood is displayed: hand-dived scallops, large, wild, shucked oysters; live jumbo shrimps and – an item that will catch your attention if available – the giant clam, also called the geoduck or mirugai. This bivalve shellfish is a unique creature, one of the most long-living species on earth; an existence of 150 years is not exceptional. The rather strange name comes from Lushootseed, from an old Indian dialect of the tribes that formerly inhabited Washington State. It means 'dig deep' and this shellfish actually digs itself deep into the sand while only its siphon, which can be up to one meter long, protrudes. Although considered a delicacy in many places, amazingly, it has only been commercially cultivated from around 1970.

Among all the other top dishes in their repertoire, the Oriental Garden team really seems to work genuine magic with the geoduck. I prefer to eat it raw, in thin slices, rather like the Japanese would prepare sashimi. The meat of the siphon has a very strong taste of the sea and a special texture; the harder pieces are lightly floured and served after being rapidly deep-fried at a high temperature. These two preparation methods bring out the purity of this remarkable seafood and demonstrate the chef's respect for this unusual produce. Oriental Garden is a grand kitchen in all its tranquility and unpretentiousness.

445

11

# NOM WAH TEA PARLOR

13 Doyers St. (between Bowery and Pell St.) - NY 10013
T (212) 962-6047 - www.nomwah.com
Open daily: 10:30 a.m.-10:00 p.m.

Doyers Street is a somewhat forgotten street in Chinatown, yet it has a rich history. Hendrik Doyer, a Dutch immigrant, had a distillery here in 1791, and between 1893 and 1911 this was the location of the first Chinese theater.

a monumental dish of pure perfection

# The original egg roll

The slightly strange bend in the road has given it the nickname 'the bloody angle' because this street was the scene of countless shoot-outs by the Tong gangs. On no other street in the US have so many people been killed.

In 1920, the Choy family opened a Chinese bakery and tea house at number 13-15. It became famous for its mooncake filling, red bean filling and almond cookies, which are still a specialty of the house. In 1968, the lease expired and the manager, Wally Tang, who had worked there since 1950 from the age of sixteen, moved the business to number 11-13. And that is where Nom Wah Tea Parlor still stands. Wally Tang bought the place in 1974; his life work is now being carried out by his family. 'Dim, ergo sum.'

Dim sum is no doubt my favorite way of eating. I have always been impressed by the speed that genuine dim sum restaurants can conjure up an unbelievable variety of tastes and forms. Everyone savors and enjoys, it is super-cozy and everyone is delighted.

Dim sum is not really a snack, as many people mistakenly think. It refers to a way of eating. Dim sum means literally 'stirring your heart'. In Cantonese, people refer to it as *yum cha,* which means 'tea drinking'. This better exposes the roots of dim sum, as it actually originates from the time of the Silk Route when many resting places were established for travelers, and where tea was served with small snacks. Many of my most heroic meals were dim sum meals: the variety, the diversity, the purity in taste sensation and especially the play on textures raises a top dim sum chef to one of the greatest culinary masters.

In my opinion, Nom Wah's dim sum is one of the best that I have ever eaten outside of China. The sui mai, the har kau, pure perfection. The egg roll is legendary and tastes insanely good. A paper-thin omelet in a tasty batter, filled with crispy stir-fried water chestnuts, Chinese celery, bean sprouts and various vegetables. A monumental dish.

12

# CHINESE TUXEDO

5 Doyers St. (Bowery & Pell) - NY 10013
T (646) 895-9301 - www.chinesetuxedo.com
Open daily: 6:00 p.m.-midnight

Doyers Street is a somewhat forgotten street in Chinatown, but it has a rich history. Hendrik Doyer, a Dutch immigrant, ran a distillery here in 1791 and from 1893 to 1911 this was the location of the first Chinese theater.

# Whole Crispy Skin Squab with Spice Salt and Black Vinegar

The slightly strange bend in the street is nicknamed 'the bloody angle' because this street was the scene of countless shoot-outs by the Tong gangs. No other street in the US has claimed as many lives. Nowadays, the Tong gangs have been replaced by hipsters and other types looking for new hotspots, and the Chinese Tuxedo is certainly not one to overlook.

Stepping into the new Chinese Tuxedo is a unique experience. Enter under the vertical neon light where the restaurant is located, and at first glance it looks somewhat chaotic, even claustrophobic as the staff tries to streamline the large number of guests. Go further in until you see the light at the end of the tunnel where the sprightly white marble tables smile at you invitingly from below as you descend the staircase to the sunken hall where the restaurant is located. Wrought iron, plaster, cement, tropical plants and dark booths constitute the interior.

The entire place exudes an air of vintage with a good dash of drama, which was most probably normal in the former theatre, which incidentally was the very first theatre on the east coast of the US. During the tense period of the Chinese gang wars, the theatre was declared neutral territory and this was about the only place where the Hip Sings and the Un Leongs sat together peacefully. That is, until an incident that occurred in 1905, when one of the parties set off fireworks which the other party misinterpreted as an attack and 'retaliated' with live ammunition.

The kitchen is run by Paul Donnelly, a Scotsman with a great deal of experience in Asian cooking. He creates his versions of Chinese classics to the delight of his guests, among them many Chinese. He calls it a type of fusion and that is what I really appreciate. With certain dishes, such as the Char Siu, the chef demonstrates that he also knows how to prepare classical Chinese dishes, and perhaps he is the best at this. A must is the whole roasted dove with a crispy skin, black vinegar and spicy salt; a perfect illustration of how very simple a delicious Chinese meal can be. Put Chinese Tuxedo on your to-do list and you are a tad richer for this beautiful experience!

Serial NO: 2763
義佛軒 佛具專門店
68A
皇上皇
66 MOTT ST.
Amazing 66 Restaurant
212-334-0099
黃金萬両

13

# AMAZING 66

66 Mott St. (between Canal St. and Bayard St.) - NY 10013
T (212) 334-0099 - www.amazing66.com
Open daily: 11:00 a.m.-11:00 p.m.

When Reinhard Löwenstein, a good friend and a top Riesling winemaker from the Mosel came to visit me, I took him to Chinatown and there in one of the typical fish stores we came across a bucket full of eyes staring at us. These were big frogs with only their eyes sticking out of the water.

amazing 66 is truly amazing

# Frog and twin rice

When we inquired where in Chinatown we could find the best-prepared frogs, the answer was of course the Amazing 66. Both of us are adventurous diners and that way we discovered the phenomenal kitchen of this top restaurant.

Helen Ng, the very proud owner, loves traditional family-style Chinese food. The menu contains predominately Cantonese specialties. The diverse varieties of frog dishes are fabulous, the dry fried frog legs are coated with a superb batter and the frog stew with chestnuts is characterized by lovely fresh frog meat. One of the showpieces is the frog and twin rice. Twin rice is a balanced, diversified rice dish consisting of six different types, in this case prepared with frog parts in order to give it an extra punch of flavor. The perfect stir-fried vegetables and the more noble parts of the frog do the rest. Wow! The twin rice is truly one of the best rice dishes I have ever eaten. The taste, the crispness and the mouthfeel illustrate the professional skill of a great chef, who is moreover challenged by a lady who knows what she wants. The result is that he has really outdone himself.

The restaurant has far more selections than just frog dishes. I was knocked off my feet by the kabocha green pumpkins, prepared whole and filled with phenomenally seasoned and slow-cooked beef. All the dishes are nicely presented and very tasty. Feel free to ask Helen for advice in selecting your dishes. Amazing 66 is truly amazing. An address you will love.

AURICCHIO
57

# DI PALO

200 Grand Street (@Mott Street) - NY 10013
T (212) 226-1033 - www.dipaloselects.com
Open Mon-Sat: 9:00 a.m.-6:30 p.m, Sun: 9:00 a.m.-4:00 p.m.

Di Palo is a conception far beyond Little Italy. The history of this neighborhood store began in 1903 when Savino Di Palo decided to change the course of his life and emigrate to the US, just like many other Italians.

# Mozzarella

## mozzarella doesn't get any better than this

This cheese maker from the small village of Montemilone in Basilicata left everything behind, including his family, friends and farm. He liked what he found in Little Italy and he opened a latteria (dairy bar) in 1910. When WWI broke out in 1914, the rest of his family joined him in NY and they decided to honor the traditions they brought from Basilicata.

Savino's daughter, Concetta, opened her own shop in 1925 on the corner of Mott and Grand, a half a block from her father's store where she sold a number of cheeses produced by her father and her husband Luigi. Two generations later, the brothers Salvatore (Sal to his friends) and Lou and their sister Marie decided to broaden the original 1903 mission of Savino. The current fifth generation is now importing top artisinal cheeses and fine cold cuts from their homeland. These are sold alongside their own cheese production, which includes caciocavallo, provolone, pecorino romano, and of course their top cheese: the best mozzarella in the world!

The word, "mozzarella" comes from the Italian verb *mozzare* (which means both "to cut" and "cut off"). For ages it has been produced in the southern part of Italy from rich buffalo milk. The term first appeared in 1570 in the cookbook of Bartolomeo Scappi.

Actually, I am not supposed to use the term mozzarella, because when mozzarella is made of cow's milk, the cheese is actually called fior di latte. In Di Palo, this is freshly made in front of you in the store; it can't be fresher than that. When I took a friendly Belgian restaurant owner, who often visits southern Italy and owns land there, around NY, I said to him: "You will now taste the best mozzarella ever." He laughed and told me that he goes to farms in Campania to taste mozzarella and buys the cheese there. How could this version of mozzarella from the center of NY come close to his? We eagerly tasted one of these mozzarellas that we bought at the doorstep of Di Palo. Although he never actually said it to me, from the look on his face I could just hear him think: "Damn, he is right." That is Di Palo for me: he makes something that everyone knows, yet makes it so well that everyone rediscovers it and asks himself why so much bad mozzarella is eaten. Di Palo is one of the NY businesses that I miss the most. I cannot thank Sal and Lou enough for their magisterial fior di latte.

15

# CHEE CHEONG FUN FOOD CART

Elisabeth St./Hester St. - NY 10013

Open daily: 7:00 a.m.-7:00 p.m.

When the streets of NY are covered with snow that just keeps falling, and you trudge your way through Chinatown, the sight of the steamy food cart, half-covered by a tarp, is a relief, a sort of light at the end of the tunnel.

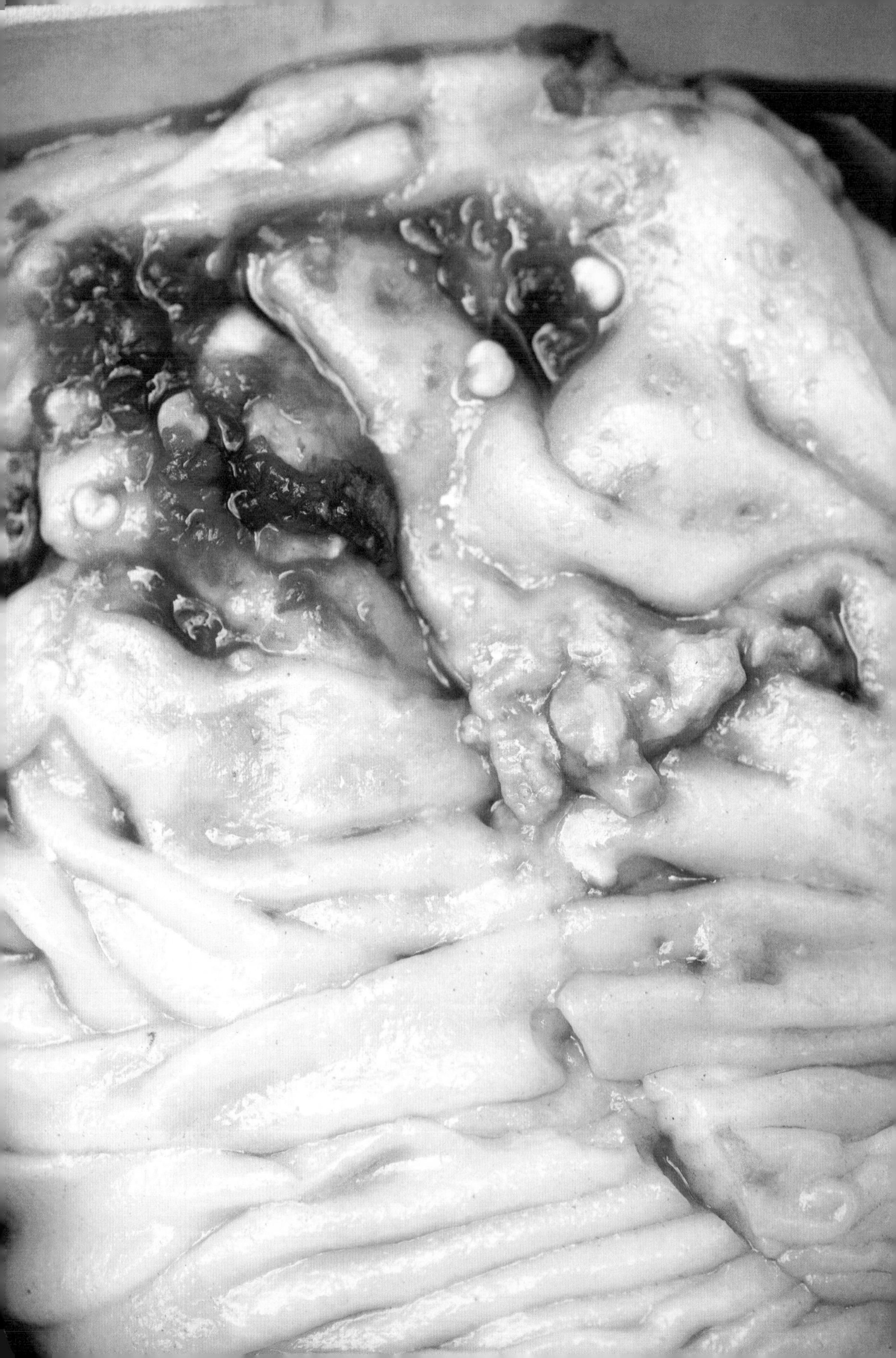

# Chee cheong fun

## cooking in the danger zone

This modest conveyance, which seems to come from one of the episodes of *Cooking in the Danger Zone* is operated by a very diminutive woman who is always up and about and is happy to conjure her hearty and tasty dishes. I call her Ah Yee, which means "small aunt". Her à la minute steamed chee cheong fun with fresh chives, pork or chicken, egg, some peanuts and soy sauce are ideal for breakfast, although I can eat it all day. Ah Yee works here from 7:00 a.m. to 7:00 p.m.

Chee cheong fun is a traditional dish from the dim sum culture of southern China and it means "noodles in the shape of a pig's large intestines." If you look at the shape, this is a well-chosen metaphor. Just like so many easy-to-prepare dishes, the subtle difference in the handling and preparation makes all the difference. A measure of rice flour, 1/4 measure of tapioca flour mixed with the same quantity of water and the fundament of your cheong fun, your runner on base, as it were, is ready. The liquid mixture is then poured into a flat steam pot especially designed for the purpose and is slowly steamed into an extremely thin rice sheet. The thinner, the better and prettier the texture. The filling is added when the noodle is nearly done so that the mixture attaches itself further around the filling and sticks to it. The thin rice sheet is than folded into thirds and sprinkled with soy sauce. The chee cheong fun of Ah Yee has a texture that reveals great craftsmanship. To be honest, it doesn't have to snow for me to make a stop at her cart.

# DOWNTOWN EAST

# ADDITIONAL EATERIES

**NARCISSA**
25 Cooper Square - NY 10003
T +1 212 228 3344
www.narcissarestaurant.com
▸ **Carrots Wellington**

17 **CHERCHE MIDI (SHANE MCBRIDE)**
282 Bowery - NY 10012
T +1 212 226 3055
www.cherchemidiny.com
▸ **Homemade Lobster Ravioli in ginger beurre blanc with piquillo peppers**

18 **ESTELA**
47 E Houston Street - NY 10012
T +1 212 219 7693
www.estelanyc.com
▸ **Gnocchi**

19 **SUSHI DOJO**
110 1st Avenue (7th Street) - NY 10009
T +1 646 692 9398
www.sushidojonyc.com
▸ **Nama tako (Live octopus sushi)**

20 **MOMOFUKU NOODLE BAR**
171 First Avenue (between 10th and 11th Street)
NY 10003
T +1 212 475 7899
www.momofuku.com/new-york/noodle-bar
▸ **Pork belly bun**

21 **CHA AN TEA HOUSE**
230 E 9th Street (between 2d & 3d) - NY 10003
T +1 212 228 8030
www.chaanteahouse.com
▸ **Tea smoked salmon**

**GOLDEN UNICORN**
18 East Broadway (between Catherine & Market Street)
NY 10002
T +1 212 941 0911
**www.goldenunicornrestaurant.com**
▸ **Siu mai**

**LOMBARDI PIZZA**
32 Spring Street (Mott & Mulberry) - NY 10012
T +1 212 941 7994
www.firstpizza.com
▸ **Pizza Margharita**

**GRAFFITI ME & YOU PRIVATE DINING ROOM**
224 East 10 Street (between 1st and 2d Avenue) - NY 10003
T +1 212 677 0695
www.graffitinyc.com
▸ **Chickpea crusted skate, mint yoghurt sauce**

**GOTHAM BAR & GRILL**
12 East 12th Street (between 5th Avenue and University Place)
NY 10003
T +1 212 620 4020
www.gothambarandgrill.com
▸ **Niman Ranch Pork Chop 41**
**Braised greenmarket kale, poached apricots, baby turnips, polenta, sage port wine reduction**

**MILE END DELI**
53 Bond Street - NY 10012
T +1 212 529 2990
www.mileenddeli.com
▸ **Ruth Wilensky sandwich**
**(house made beef salami, onion roll, mustard)**

**IL POSTO PIZZA**
310 Second Avenue (18th St.) - NY 10003
T +1 212 716 1200
www.postothincrust.com
▸ **Thin crust classica**

ISSUE 13 BOHUN YOON 4/4
CENTREFOLD MARGOT QUAN KNIGHT 1/1

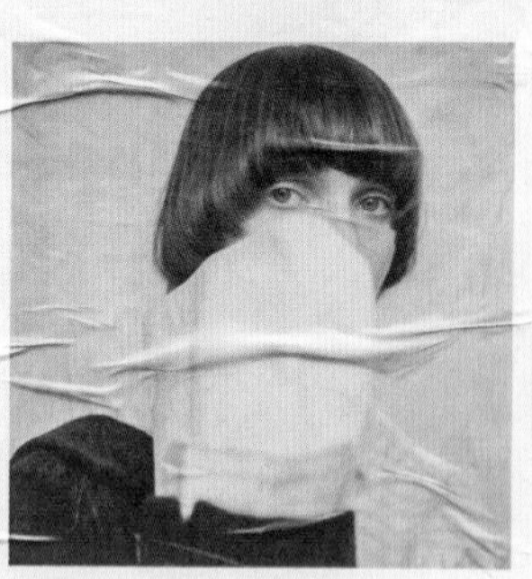

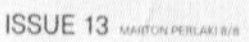
ISSUE 13 MARTON PERLAKI 8/8

MAGAZINE BOHUN YOON 3/4
BRIELA
YAN SHERIDAN
E 8 JUNE 9
Steel
Terminal 5
CHA

UE 13 PAUL KOOIKER 2/8
CENTREFOLD BOHUN YOON 2/4
MAGA
MAGAZINE LIAM HART 1/1
ISSUE 13
OMB MIÈRE
THE NEW EYE COLO AND POWDER
AVAILABLE ON

# ALPHABETICAL INDEX

## Colophon

**MARKED** is an initiative by Lannoo Publishers.
**www.marked-books.com**
**JOIN THE MARKED COMMUNITY** on @booksbymarked

Or sign up for our **MARKED** newsletter with news about new and forthcoming publications on art, interior design, food & travel, photography and fashion as well as exclusive offers and **MARKED** events on **www.marked-books.com**

**Texts:** Luc Hoornaert
**Photography:** Kris Vlegels except Babbo © *Melanie Dunea;* Buddakan © *Buddakan,* Nakazawa Sushi © *Daniel Krieger;* Eleven Madison Park © *Francesco Tonelli;* Gabriel Kreuther © *Paul Wagtouicz & Gabriel Kreuther (portrait);* Indian Accent © *Indian Accent;* Leuca © *Noah Fecks & Nick Solares;* Locanda Verde © *Dustin Aksland (portrait) & Noah Fecks;* Maialino © *Matt Duckor, Ellen Silverman, Liz Clayman, Eric Schwortz & Peter Garritano (Must Eat);* NoMad @The NoMad Hotel © *NoMad;* Saxon & Parole © *Melissa Hom & Erin Gleeson (Must Eat);* The Spotted Pig © *Amy Hou (portrait), Zoran Jelenic (interior) & Clay Williams (Must Eat);* Union Square Café © *Rockwell Group - Emily Andrews (interior) & Liz Clayman (Must Eat)*
**Graphic design:** Grietje Uytdenhouwen
**Illustrations:** Emma Thyssen
**Cartography:** Elke Feusels
**Translation:** Bracha De Man

Special thanks to Heather & Kim! 'In aeterna gratitudine to Randall Grahm'

If you have any questions or comments about the material in this book, please do not hesitate to contact our editorial team: markedteam@lannoo.com


ISBN: 978 94 014 4385 2
Registration of copyright: D/2017/45/244
NUR: 440



**#AREYOUMARKED**

RADIO CITY
MUSIC HALL
GUGGENHEIM
HONEY

RADIO CITY
MUSIC HALL
GUGGENHEIM